85531

WITHDRAWN FROM
THE LIBRARY

UN
W

D1337268

ACCESS

KA 0012659 4

Urban Policy–Making

Urban Policy–Making

Influences on County Boroughs in England and Wales

NOEL BOADEN

Department of Political Theory and Institutions,
University of Liverpool

CAMBRIDGE
At the University Press 1971

Published by the Syndics of the Cambridge University Press
Bentley House, 200 Euston Road, London NW1 2DB
American Branch: 32 East 57th Street, New York, N.Y. 10022

© Cambridge University Press 1971

Library of Congress Catalogue Card Number: 71-158554

ISBN: 0 521 08208 0

Printed in Great Britain

KING ALFRED'S COLLEGE
WINCHESTER.

352.042
BOA   86022

 PRINTED BY Unwin Brothers Limited
THE GRESHAM PRESS   OLD WOKING   SURREY   ENGLAND

Produced by 'Uneoprint'

A member of the Staples Printing Group   (UO712)

Contents

Tables

Diagrams

Acknowledgements

Like most authors I have to acknowledge a number of debts. This book rests heavily on pioneering work undertaken by a number of scholars in the United States and Britain. In addition to their indirect stimulus I have been directly helped by a number of people. Several colleagues read earlier drafts of the manuscript and I must particularly thank Jean Blondel, Peter Walters and Ian Budge. Their comments did much to improve the text and they are in no way responsible for any remaining blemishes. More than any of these, however, I must thank Robert Alford, who introduced me to this area of analysis and has continued to stimulate my efforts.

Somewhat more mundanely I am grateful to the Social Science Research Council who financed the study of which this book forms a background part. Jan Edwards typed the manuscript and coped with many other problems as they arose.

Above all, my wife and daughter provided material and spiritual support on the many occasions when both were necessary.

Introduction

Many of the most urgent problems of our time occur within our urban areas and have to be dealt with by local authorities largely created in the nineteenth century. Any solution of these problems will depend upon our understanding how the present system works. Often this understanding is seen in terms of the formal structure and processes of local authorities. At other times it appears to turn on the interplay of personalities and the impact of particular individuals. This book is an attempt to get somewhere between these two positions, to appreciate the impact of formal characteristics, and to understand the constraints placed upon individuals.

In doing this it has been necessary to examine the conduct of local authorities at a very general level. Local government seldom makes 'news' and takes very few major decisions. It does, however, expend enormous resources and affects most of our lives each day, through services like education, health and transport. Decisions about these services are taken in a routine way on most occasions, but their effects are still extensive. Accordingly, expenditures on a range of services have been examined to try and establish some of the normalities and routines underlying them. American experience suggests that this is one way to examine what are in effect 'non-decisions'.

The explanation of different levels of expenditure has been sought in the varied characteristics of each authority. Central control is a general external constraint, but it is argued in Chapter 2 that it leaves a good deal of discretion to individual local authorities. This conflicts with the usual view taken of local government but is quite in line with the variety and lack of competence often observed in central departments. In any event, variations in local expenditure are large enough to support the view that local characteristics may account for some of them.

The choice of the characteristics which explain local policies relies heavily on American research and on the inherent nature of the services being examined. Although the selection of appropriate indicators is never easy, the state of our understanding of local government justifies the use of approximate measures in some cases. This was equally true for the Royal Commission on Local Government Research which adopted a similar approach to ours. Perhaps this is most obvious in our use of Labour Party membership of local councils as indicative of disposition, a feature ignored in most writing on the subject. Though it does not reflect the subtle variations between local Labour Parties it does show strong relationships and draws attention to neglected areas of analysis.

As an aid to the selection of appropriate indicators the local authority is treated as a political system in its own right. Its various characteristics are then treated as _needs_ requiring to be met, _dispositions_ about appropriate local action, or _resources_ with which to undertake such action. The interaction of these three elements is examined for each of eight local services, revealing important variations among them. Some respond more readily to need than others, and some are much more subject to party pressure. At least one service is marginal to most of our measures, suggesting that it may be most susceptible to the efforts of a dynamic chief officer or chairman. Together they confirm the complexity of urban government and the difficulty of finding a rational solution to the problem of local government structure.

In a period of doubt and uncertainty about the future shape of local government it seems necessary to draw some relevant conclusions from the analysis. While admittedly crude in many of its aspects it does suggest profitable directions for further work and for change. The relevance of party is clear both in terms of the direction of service spending and of the operation of the local authority. Any reorganisation which produces clear control for either main party will have obvious implications. Similarly, if reorganisation results in marginal political control, as seemed possible in several Redcliffe-Maud authorities, it would frustrate much local action.

This examination also confirms the low level of public involvement and impact on service decisions. It does not follow that the solution must lie in the extended use of local elections or of other means of involvement. Unless these are virtuous in themselves, their major purpose must be to engage the local authority with the needs of those involved or represented. This may equally be done by changes on the part of local authorities. Instead of waiting for demands to be made, they might investigate the incidence of needs for various services. This need not stop at the level adopted here. Local authorities might collect original information about needs and about public dispositions and allow both of these to affect decisions. This would reduce the impact of party to some extent but would enhance the degree to which needs are met.

On the question of resources two facts emerge. One is that no system of local finance seems likely to obviate the need for central equalisation schemes. An important element of income redistribution is involved in this process and, given regional variations, seems likely to continue. At the same time, the central piper does not call the tune as much as is often supposed. His contributions permit local needs to be met and local dispositions to have more latitude. An alternative system could very easily produce severe territorial inequalities. Locally raised revenues are not essential to local autonomy, though of course central attitudes could change.

These are not offered as certain conclusions, but as suggestions which might repay more attention. This is only a first exploration of ground which seems likely to prove fertile both for political research and ultimately for an improved system of local government.

1 Approaches to the Community

Local government has recently received unprecedented attention from both politicians and academics(1) and this is a convenient time at which to stand back and assess the operation of the system and the emphases which have been applied to its study. A review of the literature on local government suggests that our knowledge is limited and an inadequate basis for the thoroughgoing reorganisation of the system which has been proposed. The substantial volume of research currently under way may do something to remedy this state of affairs, though there are signs that much of it falls within the traditional framework of local government studies of limited value.(2) This general inadequacy may be due in part to the fact that many social scientists have accepted the prevailing attitude among both students and some practitioners that local government is intrinsically uninteresting and perhaps substantively unimportant. They have accepted the thesis of centralised government in Britain and have chosen to examine central government, paying little attention to the work of local authorities.

This has meant that much of the work done in the field, itself limited in quantity, has been promoted by government or by others with an 'interest' in the current system.(3) Whether this interest is favourable or unfavourable to the existing arrangements, the general orientation has obvious implications for the questions asked and the techniques used to answer them. This is most apparent when one compares the proportions of work devoted to understanding or explaining the system with that devoted to formal description or to elaborating proposals to 'improve' the existing arrangements in accordance with the writer's values or interests. In fact there have been studies of local communities, though these have not usually had the local authority as their major focus. None attempt a thoroughgoing account of the processes of policy formation in the local authority, though some approach much closer to this than others.(4)

The absence of hard knowledge about local government implicit in these comments has two consequences. It facilitates the making of recommendations for change as the available information permits a good deal of flexibility. At the same time, it imposes limitations on action, as decision is difficult in the absence of adequate and conclusive evidence, particularly where many interests are inevitably in conflict. The fate of the Redcliffe-Maud Report is a further example of the problem.

In fact one outstanding feature of the local government literature is the prescriptive tone of much of the writing.(5) Prescription of itself is not a bad thing, but creates difficulties when it arises out of a priori assumptions about the system or is based on rather flimsy evidence. Part of this tendency to prescribe is the direct result of the circumstances in which work was carried out. Some of it was explicitly designed to make recommendations for changes in the system. In other cases the researchers themselves seemed convinced that local government was becoming extinct and argued as though their major task was to save it from such extinction. This gave a stimulus to prescription which in retrospect seems detrimental to research effort.

It is not this prescriptive tendency by itself which is harmful, but its association with other preoccupations of a limiting kind. One such characteristic, not surprising in Britain, is the preoccupation with the formal legal-institutional arrangements of local authorities. The number and areas of authorities and the complicated hierarchical structure within counties are dealt with repeatedly. The legislative basis of the whole system is discussed at some length, with increasing stress being laid on features such as the doctrine of ultra vires.(6) The formal distribution of powers is outlined together with exhaustive catalogues of services which authorities may, and invariably do, provide. These are, however, little more than lists of functions and do nothing to clarify the wide diversity concealed behind the formal façade.

What is not investigated, or less often at any rate, is the way in which legal powers are utilised and the extent to which legislative criteria may be satisfied by widely varying kinds and qualities of service. This is of vital importance given the absence of specific guidelines in much of the legislation or the tendency to legislate for minimal provision.(7) The duty of certain local authorities to provide schools is well known, as is the formal influence of the Secretary of State in local education. Little is known, however, about the variations between, and within, local school systems and the causes and consequences of such variations. Similarly with the two-tier administration of counties. Much has been written about its merits and demerits, but the only close assessment of its impact reveals the lack of strong basis for any firm judgement.(8) Current thinking seems to be against second-tier administration, but the evidence is by no means conclusive.

This catalogue of particular emphases and omissions could be continued for many areas within the legal-institutional context. Given the rather traditional orientation of many students they are almost certain to appear. A further characteristic of the literature, which may also grow out of the traditional view, is the tendency to highlight the 'problems of local government'. One example of this tendency may suffice. It involves W. A. Robson's treatment in 'Local Government in Crisis'(9) a title with obvious connotations, of the whole question of local finance, but most particularly of the implications for local authorities of the ratio between central grants and local rates. No evidence is produced about the substantive changes caused by the increasing proportion of central grants, but that increase is observed to be undermining local autonomy by providing central government with increasing capacity for control.

The only evidence which is produced, apart from the details of changing rate/grant ratios, relates to the views of Local Authority Associations about such ratios, and these directly contradict Robson's own view.(10) They do not see any danger in a greater proportion of central finance. This presents no problems for Robson, however, as such views are only being cited as evidence of the unwillingness of the Associations to recognise implications in rate/grant ratios which he can detect. Local authorities and their associations are 'short-sighted', the County Councils Association in particular showing great capacity for self-deception, and all have 'failed to understand the political advantages of enlarging the basis of local taxation'.(11) This is not the point at which to judge the issue, one point of what follows being to test the evidence for each of the positions. In the absence of such tests both positions are equally tenable, and one's choice becomes a matter of value judgement. One potential danger in such a position is clear from Robson's work. Having adopted a particular view he himself makes certain evidence to the contrary inadmissible. He talks of ministerial attitudes towards the local tax base being the product of 'a conscious or unconscious desire to keep them [local authorities] in leading strings'.(12) In other words, any failure to admit this as their aim merely reflects a lack of conscious self-awareness on the part of officials.

In addition to the absence of knowledge about many features of the system, there is an apparent unwillingness to investigate some questions. Simplifying somewhat, and ignoring some exceptional work, (13) local finance, local areas and functions, and central-local relations have been the predominant concerns. This limited perspective is a greater handicap than it might be because of the rather formal legal-institutional approach of the work in these areas. Local finance and areas and functions are important, but not all-important, and there is some doubt as to whether they have always been treated in the way best suited to revealing their importance. In some ways, in fact, it is almost possible to see all of this work as in some way derived from the preoccupation with central-local relations, and more will be said on this below.

Concern with local finance has led to the lengthy consideration of alternative sources of local income,(14) with much less study of the potential elasticity of the rate as an income source, or of its different use by different authorities. The overriding concern, as it was with Robson, has been to seek financial independence from the centre. This is expected to follow from a reversion to ratios of centrally to locally derived income like those of the 1930s. As we have seen there is some doubt about the implications of such ratios, and this view tends to ignore the transformation in the economic system since the war.

Questions immediately arise about the consequences of different income sources, as well as about the rating system itself. Does the source of money necessarily control the way in which it will be spent, and if so, to what degree? Would local authorities spend differently from the way they do at present if the bulk of their finance was provided from local sources, and, if so, on what services? Would the imposition of new local taxes modify public reactions and would this affect policy? Tentative answers to some of these questions are suggested by examination of discretionary use of rate-levying powers, like those for arts and entertainment. It would be unfair to take these as indicative of any local attitude towards major services financed in this way. What they do show is the need for more information about the significance of sources of finance before any decided stand is taken on the central-local issue.

On the issue of rates themselves, there is some evidence about their impact on ratepayers,(15) but no extensive analysis of their application by local authorities,(16) or about the potential of the tax, should one wish to exploit it. The tax is clearly regressive and this may have important implications for its use, but is not of itself a sufficient reason for condemning the tax. As has been observed, one important complication is that local financial resources are often judged in terms of their capability in the context of a desired balance between central and local contributions. If the aim is to find some local income capable of providing sufficient revenue to reduce dependence on central funds, then the rate is almost certainly inadequate. If, on the other hand, the aim is to provide only a part of total revenue from local sources, then the rate on property may well be adequate. It may be that established attitudes towards the use of the rate by local authorities are as important as the nature of the tax itself. The elasticity of the rate levied may be reduced by an objective appraisal of the impact of an increase, or by a subjective 'anticipation' of public reaction.(17) Left with discretion over some new tax, local authorities would perhaps vary as widely in their exploitation as they do now. Any subsequent attempt at equalisation would simply be a blow at the local discretion which is seen as a most desirable feature of a modified tax system.

There is now a wide variation in the rate levied by local authorities, in part as a result of their different taxable capacity. Thus one finds an obvious tendency for the rate to fall as the per capita rateable value rises. However, this general tendency hides a good deal of variation, and there is also wide variation in the amount of rate income raised per head of population. Thus while authorities are affected by the basis of the only tax available to them they are also influenced by the amounts which they wish to spend. There are authorities which levy low rates, in spite of having low rateable values, with their resultant revenue being well below the average.(18) It is of course difficult to determine whether expenditure decisions dictate rate levels, or vice versa, but an examination of local authorities reveals widely varied practice. Certainly there is evidence to suggest that this form of tax could be exploited much more than has hitherto been the case, in spite of its inherent properties.

Like finance, the question of allocation of functions among local authorities has suffered from a preoccupation with the loss of functions to central government, and with how to avoid further loss. The loss of public utilities and of the hospitals is well charted, and is often cited as evidence of more general central ambition. This preoccupation among students has tended to withdraw attention from what is left with local authorities, perhaps contributing to the lack of public interest in local elections. More than that, however, it has meant that attention tends to be devoted to keeping services in local hands, rather than to considering where they might most appropriately be controlled.(19) One result is a lack of knowledge about the many services for which local authorities are responsible. Political scientists have tended to follow the legal-institutional question of which authority performs which task, and of how functions should be allocated formally. This discussion has been marked by the absence of firm evidence on performance with the issue of local status and its functional implications looming large. Little effort has been devoted to discovering the desirability, or the cause, of

4

variations between authorities in terms of services, with the result that any rational re-allocation becomes difficult.

Where such efforts have been made the traditional explanatory variable has been population size, though current evidence shows it to have a varied effect and often no apparent effect at all.(20) This preoccupation with size is partly produced by the tendency, already referred to, to seek means by which local autonomy might be developed, large authorities being assumed to be more independent of central government. In part it is also produced by a preoccupation with largely administrative concerns where efficiency is the major yardstick, and where economies of scale are invoked as the solution to many problems. Satisfactory examination of this issue is important but is also difficult. The tendency for it to dominate much discussion is perhaps caused by the much greater difficulty presented by analysis of other questions of democracy or public involvement. This is usually seen as the major alternative criterion by which local government might be judged and the choice between them is rendered more acute by the fact that they tend to work in reverse directions. Economies of scale in terms of administrative efficiency tend to produce diseconomies in terms of democracy and participation.

A further explanation of the preoccupation with size is that political scientists have been seeking solutions to the failings of the local government system. Had they been seeking explanations for what local authorities actually do it is likely that they would have considered a number of factors other than size. Indeed it may also be necessary to ask about what is done before one asks about how efficiently it is done. Efficiency is of course relevant, but what happens is just as important as whether it happens efficiently.

Closely related to the question of size, is the question of area, which, as the Local Government Commission recognised,(21) cannot be dealt with in isolation. Implicit in their view was the idea that area and function must be considered together, though two different arguments may give rise to such a view. One is the traditional argument by which status and function were related, with area and status being similarly interdependent. Thus county borough status was sought and granted when the population reached an appropriate figure (100 000 most recently), with the functional responsibilities following almost without consideration as to their relevance. The other argument would be that certain areas are relevant to the performance of certain functions, and that this coincidence should determine their allocation. Both arguments relate closely to the issue of size, but the second acknowledges more fully the complexity with which the notion of area is endowed. Area is not simply a matter of extent or population size, in spite of the traditional view. It is also related to the economic base, social composition, age and nature of a community. The introduction of such factors into the notion of area, gives it much greater significance, though also making it much more complex to analyse.

This complexity and its relevance were very apparent in the controversy over the proposed extinction of Rutland County Council. Judged in traditional size and areal terms it was not a viable autonomous unit, but the case could not be sustained on those grounds alone. More complex considerations

5

were invoked and the absence of firm knowledge made it difficult to challenge the County's claims authoritatively. A rational assessment was not made, but perhaps it would not have been even with more evidence. Indeed the existence of such a rational case would have put a number of other local authorities under threat. Rutland's major deficiency related to the traditional size criteria. It was too small, perhaps for service viability, certainly to retain its independence from the central government. Its continued existence raises interesting questions about the validity of such a view.

A further issue in the context of size, area and function has been the pressure to simplify the whole local government structure. The large number of authorities and the complex relationship between counties and districts are often seen as militating against popular understanding and involvement. While simplification and clarification may both be laudable aims, there is not much evidence about the relation between structure and popular interest and involvement. What there is raises some doubts about the benefits of any change. Nor is there much evidence about the impact of a complex structure on other questions, such as service provision, professional competence among officers or party conflict. It has already been indicated that the optimal definition of area is complicated and it may be that some two-tier system would be most appropriate to cater for a diverse range of services, whatever its popular implications.(22)

It has been evident in talking about these substantive concerns that relations between central government and local authorities figure prominently in each discussion. Some of this preoccupation with central control may be traced to the recurrent 'theoretical concerns' of students of local government. W. J. M. Mackenzie's review of such concerns(23) brings out very clearly the concern with central-local relations as well as stressing that local self-government has become one of the 'inarticulate major premises' supporting the system. This must also be read against his review of the history of varied centralising and localising tendencies since 1830. It is interesting against this background of tension between centralising pressures and localising pressures, to consider two general views of the function of local government.(24)

> 'The first sees local authorities as mediating between central departments and the people who receive government services and controlling the local officials who administer them, a role which must be performed by an elected body.
>   The second sees local authorities as pressure groups acting on central government and the central bureaucracy as representatives of consumer interests.'

Neither of these functions is altogether compatible with Mackenzie's observation that in some sense or other local self-government is now part of the English constitution, the English notion of what proper government ought to be.(25) The first emphasises the subordinate position of local authorities while the second sees them simply as an element in central government. Both reflect closely the view of Britain as a homogeneous country which naturally gives rise to a unified and centralised system of

6

government. Indeed it is such a view that gives rise to many of the pre-occupations dealt with above. It may even account for the low public interest in local government, a rational reaction in a highly centralised system.

It is our contention that another view is equally tenable given the fact of the current system. Local authorities can be studied as 'authoritative allocators' within defined but reasonably wide limits. If one looks at them, not as adjuncts or agents of central government, but as independent governments in their own right, different orientations become possible and new questions suggest themselves. Aspects of government and politics which have normally been studied in national systems become relevant at the local level. The greater number of units of analysis available makes more sophisticated techniques possible and insights can be obtained into politics at other levels which are less amenable to research.

Support for such a view comes mainly from the United States, which may have prevented its early adoption in Britain. The same reticence would apply to many other areas of political analysis.

It is, of course, understandable in the United States, partly because of its federal arrangements and very strong traditions of local autonomy; partly, however, it is also due to the developments which have taken place in the study of politics, and the wish to develop these in a suitable research setting. Local government provides more units of analysis at the governmental level and also an extensive and perhaps more available array of sub-units. For whatever reason, it is rewarding to examine the American literature for its implications for Britain. The volume of literature is extensive and many lessons might be drawn. In the context of what has already been said about English local government, however, two general lessons are of particular importance. One concerns the substantive questions which have been considered, questions which have considerably changed over the past ten years. A number of these have already been mentioned, including a more detailed analysis of the main features of an area and their impact on politics via decisions to tax and spend. The other, closely related, concerns the theoretical principles and the methods and techniques which may be used in examining these wider substantive concerns. Examination of particular decisions or issues and resultant comments on the power structure are now seen as only one line of approach. Collection of aggregate data and the use of multivariate analysis is proving equally fruitful, and permits the examination of much wider and more general questions. If for no other reason, the dearth of empirical work in Britain, a feature not restricted to local government, gives the American experience great significance. At least it may prevent major errors of omission and commission in British work.

The two main developments being considered here represent only a segment of American experience, particularly ignoring the important but somewhat arid controversy between the elitists and pluralists.(26) This is ignored in part because of its reduced relevance in the British context where formal decision-makers assume greater significance than they do in the United States.(27) It is also less relevant for what have been suggested as the less understood areas of local government and it is on these that our attention is concentrated. It is difficult at this point to determine clearly whether the change in substantive concerns preceded or followed the theoretical and methodological developments. The two are in any case closely interrelated and the substantive changes will be considered first only because they relate more obviously to what has already been said. Indeed the change in substantive concerns becomes obvious as soon as local authorities are seen as 'independent' political systems. The tendency in Britain in any work not in the traditional mould, has been to examine certain political phenomena which occur in a local setting.(28) It has not really sought understanding of the local political system as such, except in an implicit sense.

The substantive change in the United States may be summarised as the movement from concern with Who Governs? to concern with Who Gets What When How? This change of emphasis was called for very clearly in the urban context, and neatly summarised by James Q. Wilson in his observation that 'Urban politics now demands a concentration on ends and not means'. (29) Such an observation by itself has a revolutionary ring in the British context where legal forms occupy so much attention, and where what is seen to be done often appears to be as important as what gets done. Wilson, however, goes much further in spelling out what he has in mind, and already a good deal of substantive work has been done along the lines he was advocating.(30) Starting from the need to investigate outcomes he emphasised the need to investigate the system as a whole rather than the individual or group level as in the past. There is work on local groups and local parties but this seldom relates them to the system in which they exist or measures their impact on political outcomes from it.(31) In the same way Wilson drew attention to the lack of attention given to the tracing of community features and their implications for political outcomes. Moser and Scott(32) began the first part of this process and more recent studies have continued this work.(33) Unfortunately the range of variables included did not embrace important features of the political system, nor was the link to policy outcomes carried very far.

Implicit in this appeal for examination at the systemic level, and recognised by Wilson, was the need to examine outcomes in terms of regular patterns of action rather than as particular issues or decisions. He took as the essential unit of analysis 'the routine behaviour of the city as it provides certain services or as it conducts its political affairs'. This helps to meet one of the problems met in issue-oriented research which could not account for action that never came up for discussion for one reason or another.(34) In the British context the relevance of this is clear. There is a danger that more will be known about the limited issue of comprehensive reorganisation than about decisions taken in the remainder of the educational system. The inadequacy of this is obvious at the moment with controversies arising over local control of art education and the development of polytechnics. More importantly it does not fully reflect reactions to major policy suggestions, such as those of Crowther, Newsom and Plowden(35) to say nothing of the designation of educational priority areas(36) and it certainly tells us little about the disposition of the large funds spent by local education authorities. When one considers that in 1962-3 they spent £980 million on current account and £139 million on capital works, the gap in our understanding

8

becomes very significant. Both the routine and the non-routine decisions which together produce these totals need to be understood.

This appeal for a substantive reorientation coincides with the more 'scientific' approach of modern political studies. The development of more general understanding, even on a probabilistic basis, demands more than case studies of issues. It is at this point that the substantive and theoretical strands coincide and this was clear in comments made before Wilson wrote. Some years earlier Peter Rossi had summarised the dilemma of community studies, while at the same time outlining what might become the salient theoretical concerns. Going even further than those who criticise the consideration of particular issues, he argued that 'case history after case history of communities will lead nowhere and has led nowhere'.(37) This unequivocal call for comparative study of whole communities has found a full and varied response in the United States, but has not really been met in the British context. Rossi himself spelt out some of its implications and they have as much relevance in Britain as in the United States. These were:

(i)   the absence of a good conceptual scheme for identifying the crucial elements in the community structure;

(ii) the absence of knowledge about the relation between economic and ecological exigencies and social structures;

(iii) the absence of knowledge about the impingement of social structure on important social institutions, and,

(iv) the absence of knowledge of the effects of local government structure on community.(38)

The filling of such gaps which has taken place in the United States confirms their relevance, particularly for the substantive interests which Wilson has proposed. It is the relationship between Wilson's proposed dependent variables and Rossi's suggested independent variables which is of crucial importance and has been closely developed by Robert Alford.(39) He emphasises the need to relate variables at the same level when seeking explanations. In seeking the explanation of a particular decision it may be that particular decision-makers are most important. If, on the other hand, one is seeking to explain general activity in a particular field, then particular individuals have less impact and structural characteristics of the area involved will have much greater relevance.

This view is developed and Wilson's notion of policy as a dependent variable is elaborated, together with the idea of an even more general role of government. And, more importantly, Alford specifies very precisely the nature of the independent variables applicable when explaining policies and roles of government, developing a more precise formulation of the major structural and cultural determinants. Such an approach has obvious relevance as soon as one accepts local authorities as autonomous decision-makers for reasonably important purposes. Once this has been done any attempt to examine policy or the role of government demands an extension of the factors which have normally been considered relevant to the study of English local government. Problems remain, both theoretical and opera-

9

tional, but more detailed drawing on American experience can help to overcome these. In spite of differences between the two political systems, many of the concepts used and the detailed operational measures are interchangeable.

Before embarking on a more elaborate theoretical scheme for looking at local politics, it is perhaps necessary to provide some further support for the claim to local autonomy. Given that all that follows rests on this major premise, and given its novelty in the context of much writing on the subject, it will be dealt with in a separate chapter. Succeeding chapters will be taken up with the development of a theoretical model and the examination of some of the relationships to which it gives rise.

2 Variations between County Boroughs

The previous chapter suggested that there were gaps in the literature on English local government, and that American experiences indicated that a substantive focus on policy-making with its theoretical and methodological corollaries might help to fill such gaps. Before outlining a basis for applying such American experience in England, some further examination of the English situation is called for. It is necessary to test the basic assumptions which have been made about the system because, if they are accurate, any explanation of local authority activity would be better sought in Whitehall and the decision centres of central government. The justification for applying the ideas of Rossi, Wilson and others in the British context must rest on an empirical justification of the view that English local authorities are political systems in their own right. Only if they can be demonstrated to operate as autonomous units will the exercise be worthwhile. Only if they can be shown to influence governmental activity directly in their areas will they be of interest in political terms, though of course they would retain interest as factors in the decisions of central government.

Consideration of their autonomy involves consideration of some of the related factors already discussed. As autonomy is dependent on the central-local relationship, factors already cited as relevant to this should also be introduced. Finance and size would seem to be the two principal ones, as the traditional view sees these as relevant to local autonomy whatever the general picture might imply. All authorities are tightly controlled, but some are more tightly than others.

Adopting for the moment a traditional position, a number of hypotheses may be generated from the implicit theory involved, which has been briefly summarised. Though the theory is not explicit enough to make precise formulation and testing possible, an attempt will be made to bring empirical evidence to bear on such hypotheses. The five hypotheses to be tested here are:

Hypothesis one: Local authorities within any particular class of authority will display broadly similar levels of activity within any service area because of the operation of central pressures and controls.

This hypothesis derives from the general stance of much of the literature which has been referred to earlier. Thus W. A. Robson observed: 'Local authorities have become subservient to the central government', (1) or talks of them as 'mere administrative agents'. L. P. Green adopts a similar view, observing that even major authorities have become 'virtual agents of the central departments'.(2)

The most recent statement of this position occurs in the report of the Royal Commission on Local Government which observed of the relationship:

'We do not believe that the right relationship exists today—or could exist while there are so many local authorities of such diverse sizes, and local government is unable, because of the defects in its structure, to play its proper role. What is wrong in the relationship at present is partly that central government tries itself to do some of the things that belong properly to local government, and partly that local authorities are not given enough freedom to go their own way.'(3)

Hypothesis two: Within any class of local authority, the smaller authorities will be more likely to conform to central wishes and submit to central control.

Hypothesis three: Within any class of local authority the smaller authorities will be less able to sustain above-average levels of service because of the effective inadequacy of such authorities.

The second and third hypotheses derive from the most widely held view about central-local relations. The most recent study devoted solely to this subject made the point very clearly.

'The difference in the size of local authorities inevitably creates many differences in their relations with government departments. At one extreme the four county boroughs and eighteen counties with populations of over 500 000 are able to employ such large and highly qualified staff, have programmes of such dimensions, and are so well known in the departments that their wishes inevitably carry great weight... The county boroughs and counties at the other end of the population scale are in a very different position... Clearly their relations with the departments are affected by the relative inexpertness and lack of qualifications of their officers and members, and by the poverty of their resources.'(4)

This clear statement of the difference in relationship with small and large authorities found a major echo in the Royal Commission. Much of the research was exclusively devoted to examination of the impact of size on local authority work, largely it seems determined by the assumed relationship between independence and size.

Hypothesis four: Within any class of local authority, poorer authorities in terms of financial resources will be more likely to conform to central wishes and submit to central control.

Hypothesis five: Within any class of local authority, poorer authorities in financial terms will be less able to sustain above-average levels of expenditure because of their dependence on central funds and the difficulty of using such funds for abnormally high spending.

The final two hypotheses are again well supported in the literature. Robson's assertion about local subservience arises 'mainly but not entirely because of their [local authorities'] excessive dependence on central grants'.(5) As long ago as 1956, the Royal Institute of Public Administra-

12

tion formed a study group to consider local sources of revenue. Their suggestions rested very much on the substance of these two hypotheses and their agreement that:

'For a number of years the trends in the source of their finance have been in the wrong direction; and that the time has come to halt these trends, and to seek new sources of revenue which will reduce, rather than increase, the dependence of local government upon government grants and give back a greater measure of financial independence to local authorities.'(6)

Central finance and local autonomy are clearly seen to be incompatible and this assumption deserves rigorous testing.

There is, of course, close interrelation between these hypotheses, but the first is most crucial for our purposes. If it is supported and the case for general central control established, then the others remain of interest but become somewhat academic. Uniformity of service is implied in the first hypothesis and empirical support of it would provide at least strong prima facie evidence for central control. Local factors could give rise to uniformity but the diversity of English cities and counties makes this unlikely. On the other hand, if the hypothesis is rejected, this will not necessarily mean the absence of central control but will mean that some service variation is likely to be explained by non-central factors. The underlying assumption in this and the other cases is that central control makes for uniformity of service. This seems a reasonable assumption even if one accepts Griffith's point that 'the impulse behind the fixing of minimum standards is not primarily a desire for uniformity... but more simply that the departments do not trust all the local authorities'. (7) The result is a pressure for uniformity, whatever the intention.

Table 2-1 presents data to test the first hypothesis. Similar figures could be shown for county councils, but the aim here is to concentrate attention on county boroughs. This decision arises out of the fact that they are the only local authorities providing the full range of services. They can thus demonstrate service variation across a range of services which gives some check on the variation in the effectiveness of central control between services. (8) Secondly, county boroughs, being more compact, permit the use of techniques less adaptable in county terms. Also they display more developed political machinery in many cases which makes their study more revealing in the broad sense. Finally, the very fact that they are urban authorities enhances their interest. It is in an urban setting that increasing numbers of people live their lives, and where most of the major problems of local government are presented. (9)

Examination of the table supports rejection of the hypothesis. Looking simply at the range of expenditure within each service the extremes are very wide apart. This is re-emphasised by the standard deviations which show very high values, though varying between services. The individual cases quoted do no more than confirm this more general evidence, both at the quartile points and in the groups of extreme authorities. Indeed the table supports rejection both of the general factor of control, and the idea that such control takes away the major peaks and troughs of expenditure.

13

Table 2-1. Range of spending per 1000 population for selected services in County Boroughs (in £)

	Welfare	Children	Health	Education	Library
Highest	1847	1272	3152	28 093	1233
	1752	1224	3017	28 049	1083
	1550	1167	3017	27 382	963
	1492	1159	3008	27 105	958
	1472	1132	3000	27 061	950
03	1234	873	2424	25 442	764
H1	1021	747	2179	23 970	679
Q1	869	625	1942	22 817	581
	657	450	1629	19 548	475
	653	409	1624	19 490	444
	652	408	1620	18 829	436
	551	335	1534	18 464	430
	540	138	1507	17 263	406
Mean	1044	748	2200	23 970	689
Standard Deviation	263	211	373	2100	150

Note: The figures quoted in the table refer to the total of expenditure met from all sources per 1000 population, and are taken from the series of service details published by the Institute of Municipal Treasurers and Accountants and the Society of County Treasurers.

These figures relate to expenditure on different services and may not be altogether indicative of the actual variation in provision of services. This point will be taken up in detail later (10) but for the moment two factors are worth comment. The expenditure pattern on each service covers a wide range of features of the service, including administration, and for compilation purposes is relatively standardised between authorities. Expenditure on these different aspects of each service is of course varied and this variation is important. The main concern here, however, is with the broad variation in service totals, as many of the detailed differences are only explicable in much more detailed terms. The other factor is the growing observation of substantive service variation in various fields. Such observations give strong support to the significance in provision terms of the range of expenditure noted here.

For example, Julia Parker has dealt in descriptive terms with a number of major variations in children's services, both in terms of provision and of staffing. (11) Similar degrees of variation are reported in Elizabeth Layton's work on local authority building. (12) Though not always widely remarked the traditional variation in grammar school places between different

14

authorities was considerable, and may even account for some of the pressure to comprehensivise. In terms of the latter development a wide diversity exists, though this may simply be a product of differential timing of the introduction of such schools, rather than a permanent inequality in provision. This catalogue of variations could be repeated for many other services, though it is acknowledged that the degree of variation differs between the services. The point is that there is considerable variety, and that such variety is not consistent with the degree of central control traditionally observed.

Turning to the second and third hypotheses, concerning the effect of size on performance and on central-local relations, evidence is more difficult to obtain. This is particularly so in the case of submission to central control, where it is not always possible to be sure how the relationship between the centre and the localities was worked out.

Where local authorities agree with the central government this need not imply central control. The coincidence of interest may secure compliance with central wishes on the part of local authorities. Equally, when they do not comply this may be in defiance of central wishes or be acceptable to the centre. As before, it will be assumed that the centre wishes for reasonable uniformity, and this assumption underlies the data used. The first test utilises the expenditure pattern of the smaller county boroughs, among the five services already considered. This serves as a test of both hypotheses, but to secure an improved examination of the second, reactions to the demands of 'Circular 10/65 on Comprehensive Schools' will be considered. (13) This contained explicit central requests and reaction to it gives some indication of willingness to defy the central government. The Education Bill now (1970) proposed by the Labour Government, compelling comprehensive reorganisation, indicates the strength of the claims behind the circular, just as the time-lag before its introduction suggests some reticence about central dictation.

Table 2-2 shows the rank order among all county boroughs of the twenty smallest authorities, in terms of the five services already considered. It will be seen that for each of the services almost half of these authorities fall in one of the extreme quartiles. For the children's service as many as twelve of the authorities fall into these extremes, though here it must be noted that only three of those are in the highest quartile. This raises the question of whether central government is more concerned at any deviation from the average, or only at deviations in one direction. The comments of J. A. G. Griffith cited earlier suggest that low spending may be their main concern, though here we have argued the more general case that they are concerned with deviations above and below the average. The data here offer comment on both types. There are considerable deviations from the average and the general case for central control does not seem tenable in the face of such evidence. These deviations divide fairly evenly above and below and would tend to support rejection of either of the more particular claims for central control, that it forces low spenders up, or high spenders down.

Looking at these particular county boroughs, all except two show extreme placements on at least two services. Five out of the twenty authori-

Table 2-2. Rank of the twenty smallest County Boroughs on selected services based on per capita spending

	Welfare	Children	Health	Education	Library
Lincoln	17	48	11	59	5
West Hartlepool	79	40	54	15	60
Warrington	52	6	14	58	27
Barnsley	7	73	17	23	55
Carlisle	73	67	41	11	51
Tynemouth	40	36	76	31	30
Gloucester	66	39	23	1	19
Hastings	55	44	71	76	63
Worcester	12	13	61	50	81
Barrow-in-Furness	58	30	32	63	41
Dudley	54	66	46	64	23
Wakefield	21	70	26	21	45
Eastbourne	20	78	50	79	12
Bury	61	69	68	74	58
Chester	46	41	70	57	16
Merthyr Tydfil	22	77	19	8	49
Great Yarmouth	33	65	44	36	9
Dewsbury	14	9	16	6	46
Burton on Trent	27	46	52	7	66
Canterbury	75	79	66	67	57
Number falling in an extreme quartile	9	12	10	12	8
Number falling in highest quartile	5	3	5	6	5
Number falling in lowest quartile	4	9	5	6	3
Number spending above average	9	6	9	10	8

ties show such placements on four out of the five services. Small authorities not only defy central wishes for uniformity, but do so systematically across a range of services. This strengthens the case for rejection of the hypothesis as it controls to some extent for the varied quality of government departments in this context. Hypothesis two would be rejected, saying nothing for the moment about hypothesis three.

Turning to the more detailed case of comprehensive reorganisation, similar findings emerge to confirm rejection of the hypothesis. Of the ten smallest authorities just dealt with, one was already operating a comprehen-

16

sive scheme in 1966, an unusual position in itself. Three submitted plans within the year allowed by the Department Circular, but no less than six failed to do so, a higher proportion than among all county boroughs. Looking at these six authorities in 1968, two years after submissions were called for, two have had schemes approved by the Department of Education, while one scheme is under review. Of the other three authorities, one has not yet submitted, while the other two have refused to submit any scheme at all. In terms of our hypothesis it is interesting that such small authorities have been among those forcing the overt display of central control contained in the new Education Bill. The general case is reinforced somewhat by the fact that the physical problems which often delay preparation of reorganisation plans are less pressing in smaller authorities with fewer schools. This may be offset by the fact that any reorganisation in a small authority involves all the secondary schools. In large authorities some latitude is possible and parts of the school system may be omitted from an interim scheme. The example as a whole is not altogether ideal, the issue being somewhat symbolic and therefore perhaps less urgent in central government terms, though this is offset by the ability of any authority to comply in principle at no immediate cost. It is, in any case, an area in which central intentions were clear and local responses were relatively unambiguous. (14)

A test of hypothesis three is also contained in Table 2-2. It should be remembered that this hypothesis suggests that small authorities will tend to fall below the average expenditure for all authorities not because of central controls but because of local inadequacies. It has already been observed that these authorities in fact operate at very high and very low levels. While central control often fails to alter low expenditure, the inadequacies of small scale do not prevent some high spending. That this is not simply a product of diseconomies of small scale is confirmed by recent evidence. (15) The figure of such spending increases substantially if one takes above-average levels rather than highest quartile figures. The number of authorities spending above the average level ranges from eight in the welfare service to four in each of the children's, health and education services. There is some reason to suppose that this second set of figures is more appropriate in the light of comments in the literature on related matters. (16) More will be said on this question of size later, but the limited evidence here, while it may not provide a convincing rejection of the hypothesis, is by no means strongly supportive. The hypothesis remains somewhat doubtful, and will receive more detailed treatment later in the text.

The data in Table 2-3 bears on the relation of financial capacity and levels of activity postulated in the fourth hypothesis. The figures are for the sixteen county boroughs receiving the highest percentage of rate deficiency grant in 1965-6. (17) This is taken as a measure of their financial capacity, being designed to equalise local revenues and thus indicative of central assessment of local poverty. The table offers some evidence for rejection of the hypothesis, or at least for severe qualification of it as stated, again assuming deviations in either direction from the average to be less acceptable at the centre. Of the eighty possible placements of the authorities on the five services, no less than thirty-nine fall into the extreme quartile ranges. Another ten placements fall very close to the quarter and

Table 2-3. Rank of the sixteen 'poorest' County Boroughs on selected services based on per capita spending

	Welfare	Children	Health	Education	Library
Bootle	48	56	63	22	48
Huddersfield	24	33	36	27	32
Bradford	23	5	10	33	25
Bury	61	69	68	74	58
West Hartlepool	79	40	54	15	60
Blackburn	4	24	4	48	40
Hull	6	47	13	4	17
Burnley	18	60	49	29	14
Rochdale	64	38	42	14	18
Barnsley	7	73	17	23	55
Barrow	58	30	32	63	41
South Shields	25	26	15	55	61
Oldham	55	3	2	30	31
Dewsbury	14	9	16	6	46
Halifax	37	51	62	28	33
Methyr Tydfil	22	77	19	8	49
Number falling in an extreme quartile	9	7	11	7	5
Number falling in highest quartile	6	3	8	5	3
Number falling above average	11	8	10	12	7

three-quarter marks. This gives a substantial case for rejecting the general hypothesis, and this decision is reinforced when one looks at authorities rather than at services. Among these County Boroughs, several rank very high or very low on a number of services, Bury ranking very close to, or well within the lowest quartile on all services, and Oldham and Dewsbury occupying the reverse positions. Indeed only two of these authorities do not fall in the extreme quartiles on at least two services, while eleven authorities do fall there on at least three of the measures. There does not appear to be a very strong relation between lack of local resources and the spending of average amounts on services.

Using the comprehensive reorganisation example, again, it is possible to check this degree of central control in one particular area. This case should be treated with extra caution as the decision in question was essentially a symbolic one for many authorities, action being a long way ahead. (18) Table 2-4 shows the position in the sixteen authorities with low resources, defined as before, in terms of their compliance with Circular 10/65 in both

Table 2-4. Position of the ten smallest and sixteen 'poorest' County Boroughs in terms of Comprehensive Reorganisation in 1966 and 1968

Year	Operating a scheme	Submitted a scheme	Submitted and approved	Not submitted	Refused to submit
Ten smallest County Boroughs					
1966	1	3	—	6	—
1968	1	2	4	1	2
Sixteen poorest County Boroughs					
1966	—	12	—	4	—
1968	3	2	9	1	1

Note: These details are taken from the 1966 first report of the Comprehensive Schools Committee on the response to Circular 10/65 and from **New Society,** 11 July 1968.

1966 and 1968. The evidence here is much more favourable to the hypothesis about central control. Only four of these authorities failed to submit in 1966, and only one of these four had still not submitted in July 1968. One lonely exception had failed to submit at all, but this does not alter the overwhelming impression. It means that for hypothesis three the two sets of evidence tend in conflicting directions, though the detailed look at comprehensive planning already referred to suggests that the comprehensives' case is less reliable as evidence on this particular question.

Finally, the evidence on the relation between lack of local resources and incapacity for service provision is generally negative. Taking the data in Table 2-3 as the basis, on these five services no less than thirty-five of the placements are in the highest third of rank orderings. If one extends this to those falling above the half-way mark, then the figure becomes fifty. Thus it is clear that a substantial number of these poor authorities do spend above average amounts on a number of services. This may in part be due to central funds alleviating many local shortages, but the standardisation of the grant procedure suggests that local factors may well be an important contributory influence.

The major impression of this series of tests taken together is that the hypotheses should be rejected, or severely modified. This casts further doubt on some earlier claims, and confirms that the recent American experience may be more relevant to the British case than is usually assumed. Central control is less apparent in policy outcomes than might have been supposed. Variation in such outcomes is not to be explained simply by the divergent size of authorities, nor by their divergent domestic resources. It may thus be legitimate to treat local authorities, or at any rate, county boroughs, as authoritative allocators, and some of the determinants of their allocations as lying among as yet unexplored local features. The centre has a part to play in setting boundaries within which local authorities operate, but the divergence within those boundaries must be explained elsewhere. It is possible, of course, to argue that variation is not incompatible with central control. The centre may welcome diversity. Even if this is true it still leaves the determinants of such variation in the localities rather than at the centre.

It is now time to move to the elaboration of a theoretical scheme which seeks to identify those local features which do give rise to service variations within centrally defined limits.

3 A Model of the Local Political System

The first two chapters have been taken up in establishing the extent of local autonomy and some of its implications, which constitutes the basic justification for treating local authorities as political systems in their own right. It is now time to turn to the development of an explanatory scheme which will provide a productive and meaningful analysis of the local political system, both in terms of particular services, and ultimately in terms of the whole range of government activity. A scheme is needed which will impose some order on the many local features which may be relevant in the determination of policy outcomes. Factor analytic techniques might be used to produce such an ordering, as they were in 'British Towns', but they are not a substitute for a theoretical framework which would achieve the same objective.

The scheme being proposed here is that three broad aspects of any community combine to produce output, or policy, in specific areas, and that the combination of such policies constitutes the overall scope of government. Briefly the scheme suggests that activity in any service will depend on the incidence of need for that service, on the disposition of the authority to provide the service and on the availability of resources with which to provide the service. Each of these factors will be considered in turn before looking at the complex pattern of interrelationships between them.

NEED

The idea of need is commonplace and has become a standard concept in discussion of the social services. In such a context it is invariably seen in subsistence terms with a persistent struggle going on between 'progressive' attitudes and residual poor law traditions. Also it is primarily discussed in the context of income deficiency and the traditional needs for food, shelter and clothing. In fact the concept is used explicitly and regularly in the present local government system when exchequer grants to local authorities are being calculated. A number of local factors are given special emphasis by central government on the assumption that they constitute reliable indicators of the extent of expenditure which the authority will have to incur. These special factors have their primary, though not exclusive, relevance for the social services. (1)

In the scheme being proposed the concept of need will be widened and treated as potentially relevant, not just to social service areas, but to any service provided by the local authority. Initially this is confusing as it conflicts with the established usage and also to some extent with the common-sense use of the term. Unfortunately, an alternative term such as 'deficiency' carries overtones of judgement which are perhaps undesirable.

The term to be used is in any case less important than what is involved and this is better appreciated in the context of concrete examples. Thus to talk of the need for swimming pools, concert halls, town halls and theatres is unusual, primarily because they are not normally seen as necessities. It is our contention that the absence of such facilities should be seen as a need or a deficiency, and that such a view greatly assists understanding of local decisions about them, and about other services. Need then becomes an objective condition of a community which can be ameliorated by council action but in relation to which the provision of relevant service is either inadequate or, as in the cases just cited, non-existent. To avoid the many evaluative problems inherent in such a definition it is necessary to adopt a modification made possible by the comparative approach being adopted. Where the available evidence suggests that need for a service arises out of some feature of the locality, it will be assumed that the greater the proportion of that feature in a locality, the greater will be its need. This is particularly obvious in the case of the kinds of service just detailed where the criteria are absolute and the absence of a theatre is directly ascertainable and constitutes a need by comparison with those areas which already possess a theatre. It is equally relevant in terms of other services where for example the proportion of clients in different areas varies.

It is possible to look at any community and select features which are appropriate to measure need as just outlined. A more systematic view can help to refine the concept, however, and can certainly be of value when one is seeking operational indicators. Two basic dimensions are involved in the concept of need. The first of these concerns the scope of need. Needs may be conceived as arising out of some condition of the community as a whole, or of some parts of the community or of groups of individuals within it. (2) Examples of the first would include the absence of major facilities such as museums, theatres or art galleries. In such cases it may be possible to distinguish the actual users of the service and they may constitute only a small proportion of the population, but the provision is essentially community-wide and available to all. Examples of the second would be different and might include the incidence of old or handicapped people. Here the need arises out of a section of the community and may be met by providing for that section. It is not necessary to provide universally in order to cater for these particular needs with services such as meals on wheels for the elderly or house conversions for the physically handicapped. Need may thus be conceived as having a general or particular scope.

Whether the need is general or particular it may relate to a second dimension involving the basis of the need. Certain needs arise out of the physical conditions of an area. One can, for example, conceive of the need arising for some major physical provision such as a meeting hall or sports centre or a public park. On the other hand, such physical needs may be more particular, involving improvements to street furnishings in one area or to particular houses, or perhaps to community facilities for a new housing development. The point about each of these is that they arise from some physical shortcoming in the community as a whole or in some part of it. The need can be met only by some material provision.

Another kind of need altogether may arise out of the character of the population within the area. Physical decay may produce needs, but many other needs arise out of personal features. The presence of handicapped or elderly people creates a need for services to cater for them. At the same time, the need may be much more general arising out of the basic condition of the population, such as areas with relatively homogeneous populations with particular needs.

This dimension of need carries clear implications about the kind of service likely to be involved, though there are cases where the distinction is less obvious. A clear analytic distinction can be made between the needs created by bad housing and those created by those living in such housing. In practice, however, the two interact closely, though many local authorities do not effectively cater for this interaction. Thus it was necessary for the Seebohm Report (3) to draw attention to the implications of improved housing for the work of the social service departments, and to stress the need for these to be related departmentally.

These two dimensions of scope and basis are illustrated in Diagram 3-1. Dichotomising on each of the dimensions creates four possible categories of need. As the diagram shows, the hypothetical incidence of need is in the main confined to cells C and D. Broadly it is argued that personal needs are unlikely to relate to the whole community. Services with a personal component tend to relate to the particular client and may thus be administered selectively. On the other hand, physical provision is less divisible and is more often derived from the whole community. The examples quoted earlier illustrate this tendency. Outside those rather special cases, however, most other physical provision is also more localised.

The point about this detailed examination of need is that so many local needs are particular in scope. Certainly among county boroughs few are small enough, or homogeneous enough, to make universal or collective needs the most common. It is this factor which gives local services their redistributive character and makes assessment of priorities so significant. In the United States home rule has created governmental units which coincide more closely with this pattern of particular needs.(4) In Britain this has not happened and what are inter-governmental conflicts in the United States tend here to become intra-governmental. The sources of conflict are inherent in the urban condition, however, and will arise whatever the form of government.

Diagram 3-1. Dimensions of Need

Scope	Basis	
	PHYSICAL A	PERSONAL B
BROAD (general)	FEW	FEW
NARROW (particular)	C MANY	D MANY

DISPOSITION

Disposition is a most complex part of the overall scheme because it relates to a number of distinct dimensions. At the same time, different groups within an authority tend to vary in terms of these dimensions, raising important issues concerning their relative impact on policy-making. An individual's ultimate decision will rest on the relationship of the different dimensions and the ultimate authoritative decision will depend upon individual and group interactions.

Three dimensions are distinguished here as combining to produce a disposition about government action to meet needs. An individual may have opinions about desirable standards of provision and about the scale and quality of existing services. This constitutes a dimension related to the level of objective need. The gap between perceived current standards and desired levels of provision constitutes need and such perceptions obviously vary widely. In discussing the presence of 'objective need' earlier, the question of standards was ignored in favour of simple relative measures. Disposition is the factor which introduces perceptions of standards into the model. National minima have been established in many services, preventing local authorities from defining standards at too low a level, or at least from acting according to such definitions. Above such minima, however, there is wide scope for local authorities to define standards as they wish. Conflict over such definitions is often present, both within local authorities and between local authorities and central departments.

A second dimension relates to the scope of need. If needs generally occur in particular sections of any community, attitudes towards those sections assume great significance. Individuals, because of their own positions, may be expected to hold varied views about society and about particular groups within it. The traditional class division of British politics exemplifies this tendency as well as giving it institutional support in the party system. Until very recently this was heavily reinforced in electoral terms by the ward system giving rise to homogeneous electorates supporting one party or the other. Urban renewal and general population mobility have combined with low turn-out to produce more heterogeneity and less direct reinforcement. What is true of class and party divisions may be equally true of other particular sources of need and of other important agencies, such as pressure groups.

This may even apply at less particular levels, perceptions of the community as a whole varying widely.(5) The 'local' is more heavily involved in, and concerned about, the community, while the 'cosmopolitan' is oriented to many more external stimuli. Both views can affect assessments of communal needs and policy decisions about them. The formal representative system gives some support to this by charging the majority party with a concern for the whole community and not simply that section which gives it support. It is also bound up with the fact that some local policies reflect the community relating to outsiders, and this can produce local solidarity.(6)

The third dimension concerns attitudes towards the government taking action to deal with needs where they are perceived. It involves a concern with both the desirability and the legitimacy of government action.

24

Given acceptance of a condition of need, and a favourable attitude towards the needy, voluntary or commercial provision may be preferred to government action. Government action is only rarely the necessary form of provision and individuals vary widely in their approach to it.(7) This may affect particular services, education being accepted generally, though not exclusively, as an appropriate government service, while much cultural provision is not. Or it may affect the balance of provision between public and private agencies. Building by direct works' departments of local authorities is a clear case where the balance is seriously in question.

Before examining the varied groups whose dispositions interact to produce policy, it is worth observing that underlying most substantive policy decisions is an implicit attitude towards local taxation. Apart from a few purely symbolic decisions, reactions to needs have to be seen alongside their tax implications. Attitudes towards taxation may themselves result from dispositions as they have been considered. It is the adjustment or reconciliation of dispositions to tax and to spend that determines the redistributive nature of government.

Given these dimensions of disposition individuals occupy varied positions in relation to each of them. These vary according to personal preferences and ideas but are also affected by one's position within the community. Not only does this affect the attitudes held but also the degree to which they might affect ultimate authoritative decisions. The average man in the street is almost certainly less aware and less involved in decisions than the committed party activist or council candidate. Similarly, the professional officer has a different view from that of the councillor from a marginal ward. Nor are these positions static. The councillor's attitudes and impact may change when he moves from opposition to government or from back-bench to chairmanship. Similarly, the official may be affected by the degree of independence enjoyed by his department. These latter points emphasise that it is not only a question of attitudes but also of the way in which different roles are structured into local policy-making processes.

Elected representatives exercise considerable collective impact because of this. In constitutional terms they are the final decision-makers and traditionally they have exercised their control at varied levels of decision. Even where they do not exercise their full constitutional role, their position gives them great scope for influencing the level and direction of government action. At the same time, they are not full-time politicians, nor are they recruited on particularly rational grounds, with the result that other groups both inside and outside the authority assume greater significance than they otherwise might.

First and foremost among such groups are the permanent officials in the local bureaucracy. Their scope for influence is increased by the technicality of many government decisions, by the blurred distinction between policy and administration and the growing tendency to see local government as a purely administrative agency. The repeated appeal to take questions 'out of politics' is indicative of this tendency, and its non-partisan basis is very reminiscent of the municipal reform movement in the United States. Where this succeeds there is some tendency for the administrator or the professional to become the policy-maker.(8)

While both elected members and officials are important they operate within a general climate of opinion which may be more or less influential. This opinion affects policy in a variety of ways, not the least being its effect on the relationship between councillors and officers. There is a widely accepted view of the 'proper' relationship and this has a bearing on the weight to be given to various opinions, or on the openness with which they can be voiced. More particularly, the public have dispositions about governmental provision. These are structured into the system by a variety of aggregating agencies because of the problems of individual involvement. Elections and the political parties are the most direct form of public involvement. At the same time, the mass media perform this function and a wide range of voluntary associations is also active and often effective. It has recently become accepted that public attitudes deserve more weight and at least one government report has been concerned with how to achieve this in the planning field.(9)

The interrelation of the three dimensions of disposition and the basic groups involved are shown in the diagram.

Diagram 3-2. Dimensions of Disposition

Groups having dispositions	Disposition towards		
	Standard of need	Scope of need	Legitimacy of govt action
Politicians			
Bureaucrats			
Public			

RESOURCES

Traditionally resources have been conceived of in almost exclusively financial terms. This is in part a product of the fact that lack of finance does underlie a number of other factors which affect local capacity to act. It is also produced, however, by the central-local preoccupation which is often seen in financial terms. If finance were the major factor in that relationship this traditional preoccupation would be sensible, as it would serve two related purposes. Its solution might provide sufficient money to cater for desired service needs, while at the same time freeing local councils from central controls. Though, as has already been pointed out, this view of central-local relations has been overdrawn, financial capacity remains an important issue and will be treated as such here. The impact of disposition on this has just been observed, but it is also related to the nature of the local tax base and to the elasticity with which it may be used. The flow of central funds is also important, though in the model being proposed here it is treated either as a fixed external, in the case of the general grant, or as a variable outside the control of the local community, in the case of the rate deficiency grant. This complicates the analysis of resources.

Other resources should also be considered of course. Financial problems often shroud its significance, but in many services the supply of manpower is a major resource. This has been well documented in the field of social services where it acts as a serious limitation on the introduction of many important schemes.(10) The recent controversy over busmen's pay and the strikes which it caused, has tended to focus attention on the general labour situation in municipal transport which is often bad. The same is true of the police service where many large cities are acutely understaffed, with obvious consequences for morale and crime detection rates. The recent report of the Mallaby Committee reveals an attempt to document this shortage, though the remedial steps are necessarily long-term.(11)

Other services may experience different resource problems. Labour content may be small, but the availability of land may be very important. Housing and urban redevelopment generally are the main areas which come to mind, as the continuing controversy over high-rise development indicates. The absence of available land, coupled of course with severe housing shortages, has forced councils to build high rise in some areas, with serious consequences in terms of direct costs as well as indirectly for other services such as children and welfare. In the same way, the development of several areas of amenity provision is directly related to the supply of land, though this is not an exclusive relationship. Finally, and this has perhaps been more common in the United States, land availability may become important for towns which are trying to encourage the development of new industry, though in Britain the Board of Trade places severe limits on local autonomy here. Without pursuing further examples in detail, it is perhaps worth noting that flexibility may be important in many situations and that land, like any other resource, can restrict local options and reduce the range of policy choices open to councils.

This brief review has covered the main areas of resource, though raw materials would be a further example. Certainly this was the case in the post-war years in the building industry, and this did affect the patterns of building adopted by local councils.(12) Another resource not often considered, though clearly of great importance, is the administrative organisation necessary to mount certain activities. In part this is a cash problem, and in part a result of inadequate managerial skills, but it may also relate to the overall organisational structure and the machinery for co-ordinating activity. Large scale redevelopment may involve many departments inter-relating, or at least many specialisms, and this requires an appropriate administrative structure. Having made these points about other resources which may be relevant to local action, it remains true that finance can overcome them all in the long-term, if not always immediately. This in itself may justify concentration on monetary indicators, though the source of funds will not be of central importance.

GENERAL INDICATORS

Having outlined the major concepts involved in our scheme, it is now necessary to move to a consideration of operational measures of each. In doing
this two broad distinctions are important. There are certain indicators
which relate more generally to needs, dispositions and resources, and which
may well be relevant over a range of local services. There are others of
a much more specific kind which relate to particular services, but are not
more widely relevant. The second kind will be taken up when the particular
services are being dealt with. Here our concern is with the former class
of general indicators.

In terms of need we are seeking indicators which fit the two dimensions of scope and basis. The element of the community from which the
need arises is one concern, and the physical or personal nature of the
need is the other. Population characteristics are the most obvious indicators available of the need for various personal services. At the same
time, it must be remembered that physical conditions may also operate
on such services and that population and physical character are closely
interrelated in many communities. There is evidence in the American
literature, for example, that supports the thesis that differing populations
do need, and demand differing services.(13) Unfortunately, the relative
heterogeneity of most English county boroughs makes this a difficult measure to apply, depending as it does on reasonably homogeneous populations.
This does not mean, of course, that the particular population mixture will
not be relevant. On the contrary, it will be most significant in determining
the degree to which needs are visible and acknowledged in any community.
It does mean that one expects very few needs to arise from the population
as a whole, as was pointed out earlier. Our concern will primarily be with
sections of the population and the implications of their interacting needs.

Taking this as a starting point, the traditional class division in British
politics suggests a first important indicator. The presence of substantial
groups of the population in either, or both, of the extreme social class categories may be expected to create needs. The degree of conflict between
these needs will be determined by the relative homogeneity of an area.
High class groups may need certain kinds of amenity and certain basic
services, such as theatres and art galleries, or refuse disposal and car
parks.(14) Equally they may be less concerned with the scale of provision
and more with its quality or location. High class groups may be indifferent
to the scale of educational or police effort, so long as the provision of
selective school places is extensive and police patrolling of middle class
areas is reasonable. The point is that middle class groups use certain
services extensively or use particular aspects of others and may thus be
construed as creating a need for these services.

Low class groups, on the other hand, given the economic basis of class
position, create needs for an entirely different range of services. Housing,
transport and social welfare services would be more relevant to groups
such as these. (15) Again there would also be a distinction in terms of the
emphasis of services. Unlike their high class counterparts, working class

groups might need a more basic and general provision. This difference would be enhanced by their much greater numbers.

Finally, they would differ in their needs for varied taxation levels. The fact that taxes impinge relatively heavily on higher class groups (particularly in the light of their service needs) suggests that they need lower taxes in the way this concept has been used here. Conversely, the lower class groups will have few particular needs in this respect because of the lower incidence of rates on property for them. It must be remembered here that it is the objective position of these groups which is at issue. Their wishes about taxes are probably the same, both wishing for lower levels, but this would be a feature of disposition as it has been conceived.

Class composition, like all the other measures being used here, will be treated on a comparative basis. There is obviously no way with our present knowledge of adequately measuring the precise level of need created by any given population, but there is an easy relative measure at our disposal. It is being assumed here that the greater the proportion of the population in any particular class category, the greater will be the needs which are created by that category. This is reinforced by the fact that the greater any proportion, the smaller must be the impact of any groups creating conflicting needs. It should be remembered at this stage that we are concerned simply with assessing objective needs, and not with determining the degree to which they are effectively communicated or met. It would be relevant also to consider the geographical distribution of the population, but this is operationally more difficult. The concentration in any area of homogeneous segments of the population may lead to the creation of need in a more obvious and effective way than would the same proportion evenly distributed throughout a community. In the absence of readily available data on ward distributions, it has to be assumed that city-wide characteristics have fairly uniform distributions as between different boroughs. To the extent that particular distribution is significant it requires detailed study and may only be relevant to some decision level below that being considered here. Overall policy need not be changed to cope with particular local problems.

The population may also be seen in terms of other categories which relate to services in less general ways. The best established is probably the age structure of the population,(16) with its obvious implications for certain services and the way in which they are combined. Clearest of all in the case of the child population and the children's service or education, it is also present in the case of welfare and perhaps other services. Certainly there is some evidence for other relationships with age groups and these merit consideration.(17) Middling age groups may well fall into an anti-tax category, and may also present their own particular service needs. As in the case of social class groups so here the particular proportions and their combination is the major factor, though it is less generalised, and should be treated more carefully

One other factor may be worth brief consideration, though operationally it is not as yet widespread enough to be used. This is the existence of an immigrant population, now generally accepted as creating a whole range of needs and imposing a disproportionate burden on some services in particular. In general it is the same set of needs as are generated by the lower class groups, but the fact of colour may have considerable added importance. While it will not be possible to study this question directly here, the comments on a number of services which follow have clear implications for the capacity to absorb and provide for large numbers of immigrants.

Turning to the physical dimension, it is again possible to distinguish characteristics likely to create needs, both from a broad and narrow base. Broadly, the age of the particular borough is perhaps most general, with its implications for the inadequacy of the overall physical plant of the community. As with personal indicators, it is not possible to talk in absolute terms, but the relative measure would again be adequate. One could consider the age of any county borough as being indicated by its population structure over time, which would indicate the likely pressure for physical services, and the period during which this was probably met.

There are problems, however, with such a broad indicator which is indirect. One ideally needs to know that developments did occur when population pressures suggest, and also the extent to which physical capital has been renewed more recently. It may thus be helpful to consider alternative measures of a more direct kind. In the first place one might take the overall density of population as reflecting a community-wide need for certain services. One would expect to find it related to needs for highway development and housing, and for urban redevelopment in general, as well as for parks and playing fields. The figure can of course be somewhat misleading, as the existing land-use pattern can seriously modify the implications of given densities. This might be overcome to some extent by considering the degree of industrialisation and the type of domestic housing within the borough, both of which might seriously affect the implications of density. In fact these latter features may themselves be significant in creating needs for certain services, such as roads and public transport.

More narrowly based are needs which arise from two main causes. One of these is the absence of some physical amenity such as a concert hall or a museum. The other is some indicator of the physical condition of part of the existing physical capital of the community. Most obviously this would affect houses and schools, though the latter would have a very narrow service impact. The housing condition, while it has direct impact on the need for houses, may also affect other services, particularly in the social service sphere. A variety of housing statistics is available which provides indications of the quality of the housing stock. The density per room in local houses provides some direct evidence about the overall pressure for house room. Alternatively, the quality of existing provision may be assessed in terms of the amenities provided in different communities' housing stock. The absence of running water or fixed bath or inside toilet, in the aggregate, gives some idea of the overall pressure for new or improved housing.(18)

Turning to dispositions the situation is more complex, with attitudinal data being expensive to obtain directly. Extensive survey research is costly and has not been undertaken with disposition as a major interest, with the result that indirect evidence must be sought. The fact that our concern is with aggregates, and would involve more than the simple summation of individual attitudes, enables us to make some progress. Given the widespread operation of party in county boroughs, one source of politicians' dispositions is available. Party does perform a major aggregating function, both electorally and in terms of the internal machinery of the council. Parties do control group members more or less, and we can gather evidence about party composition of councils.

It seems reasonable to treat the party composition of the council as indicative of the likely group disposition of the council. There is some evidence which suggests that councillors develop independent allegiances to the committees on which they serve, which is said to militate against the effect of parties. However, this effect is usually overcome in full council, and the weight of evidence is in favour of party control, especially under Labour.

In terms of attitudinal direction, the traditions of gas-and-water socialism together with conservative concern for the ratepayer suggest the major divisions between the parties. In terms of the dimensions introduced earlier, the variation between the parties is fairly clear. At the national level the debate has continued for a long time with Labour favouring much more generous standards. Because it has been national, however, and because of obvious pressing priorities the party debate has been very much restricted to the social services. If the scope of the examination is extended the party positions may be reversed. Conservatives may be more favourable to cultural amenities than are Labour. At least this seems a reasonable view until a great many priorities have been met. The development of existing services will tend to reduce the party distinctions as it eliminates certain party priorities, and party positions will have to be modified. In the past the distinctions have been clear cut but they may not be so in the future.

While it would be foolish to suppose too much rationality on the part of the parties, it seems reasonable to think that they might respond more favourably to those groups who are seen to be their supporters. The class relationship with voting is high, as are some age-group relationships, and these groups might be expected to benefit when their respective parties are in control. In certain cases, indeed, the possible illegitimacy of this kind of relationship may lead to the universal provision of services which are consumed by only certain sections of the population. In terms of local authority services one would expect Labour to favour low class groups, the young and immigrant groups. The Conservatives would favour the middle class, the old and perhaps business interests, though the interests of the latter are less distinct in most English local government.(19)

Finally, Labour would seem more likely to favour government action as a whole. It has been the party of local innovation and of national government intervention in many areas, while the Conservatives have only slowly accepted the 'mixed' economy. The view taken here will be that Labour favours a larger role for government and a broader scope, while recognising the service priorities dealt with above.

All of this suggests the relevance of party, but this relevance will be conditioned by the degree of party control. The conditions of party control in the council will affect its willingness and ability to undertake action. It is suggested here that the higher the percentage of party members on the council, the greater will be the likelihood that party affiliation will be an important factor. Given the frequency of local elections and the relative slowness of many local decisions, it is unlikely that parties with tenuous control will pursue extreme policies. The aldermanic system is often justified because it helps to overcome this problem and provides continuity even when the electoral process is showing considerable movement. The overall party measure to be used here includes this aldermanic factor, and may thus claim fairly general validity. This claim is supported by the figures in Table 3-1. These show that the degree of Labour control is related to the length of council meetings and to the referral or rejection of items at meetings. The councils with larger majorities expedite their business and have less problems of delay over items. Though only tentative evidence this lends weight to the claim and indicates that internal dissension within established Labour councils is not too frequent.

Table 3-1. Selected aspects of council activity by per cent of Labour membership of the council

Per cent Labour membership	Length of council meetings	Number of items referred back	Number of items rejected
High	115 minutes	8	9
Medium	156 minutes	11	9
Low	196 minutes	24	14

Source: Adapted from the Survey of Local Authorities conducted for the Maud Report, vol. 5.

The use of this party indicator for councillor dispositions seems reasonable, but the attitudes of officers are less easily summarised. Officers probably do share certain common orientations towards the political system, though the evidence about their nature and direction is difficult to obtain. The civil service ethos which pervades the whole public service focuses attention on the 'responsible' politician, and the public service is notoriously under-investigated. It might be assumed that most officers have a concern for the professional values in their work, and also wish to see their sphere of work expanded and developed. This may not operate throughout an authority, however, as departments vary in the degree to which they embrace professional expertise. Thus it is obvious that the Architect differs from the Baths Superintendent in this respect, though both probably wish to see their work expanded. To assess the effect of this characteristic two measures are needed. One would indicate the degree to which departmental officers were likely to be effective in policy formulation. The other would indicate likely variations between departments.

On the second of these points, there are a number of ways in which departments might be classified to indicate the degree of professionalism within them. One obvious way would be to consider the size of departments, assuming that larger staffs are coincident with more professionalism. This would hold for some departments like Education but not for others like Architects' and Children's, where there is a strong professional component, though few staff. Some account must therefore be taken of the nature of the job done by a particular department and the degree to which it is professionalised. In these terms the more recently developed services seem likely to have low professional content, because of the shortage of trained staff, and the time taken to develop uniform professional standards. It would be possible to adopt very refined measures using staff qualifications, but these are not readily available as between authorities. The result is that this factor, though recognised as significant, will not be built into the analysis. Comments will be made, however, on the anticipated relevance of this factor as between departments when they are dealt with in detail.

On the first point, as with party it is not sufficient simply to assess the direction of attitudes and their relative strength in individual terms. Some attention must also be given to those structural characteristics of an authority which might increase officer influence, either generally or as between departments. The number of departments in an authority would be one such indicator. The creation of a large number of specialist departments, may bring co-ordination problems, but is also likely to mean that more chief officers will be pursuing a professionally based appeal for expansion of their services. This has clearly been behind many of the moves to separate Health and Welfare Department, so that welfare criteria may be pursued without reference to the more traditional and established views of Health Officers. Where various professional skills are harboured in one department, it seems likely that the Chief Officer through whom items have to be channelled will have only one of the professional skills involved. This could have important consequences, both favourable and unfavourable, for the others. It may be that the influence attributed to Chief Officers in such circumstances (20) is in part a product of such departmental arrangements.

Many other direct indicators are obvious but not available. It is not possible to examine average length of tenure of officers or the incidence of internal promotion or the past experience of senior officers, though all are important factors in the present context. Nor can one pursue survey investigations among officers, cost and the civil service attitude to their work being most obstructive. Here we will be limited to the items outlined above and hope to say something useful about the impact of officers, though recognising the urgent need for a closer investigation of the topic.

Finally, there is the difficult area of popular attitudes, which is almost impossible to operationalise on the individual level without survey data based on local authorities. Here we can simply use figures indicating the degree of local interest and involvement at the crudest level to indicate the extent of attention which councils may need to give to public reaction. Turn-out at local elections is invariably low and the variation between authorities is small, but it is one general indicator. The class composition may be another, as it is indicative of those characteristics associated with interest and the capacity to get involved.(21) Ideally some measure of group activity by localities is needed, but this is impossible in any reliable form. These problems are less important than those concerned with the bureaucracy. Our measure of party controls for popular pressure to some extent by indicating relative immunity from such pressure.

This leaves the area of resources. The combination of central and local finance complicates this somewhat, together with the different bases on which services such as housing are financed. Before looking at the financial measures, however, the other types of resources may be dealt with. Available land is the most obvious as revealed by the density of population. This measure must be taken together with the pattern of land use, however, as extensive industrial use or recreational areas can lower densities somewhat artificially, creating a somewhat inaccurate comparative statistic. Manpower details are more difficult to obtain for individual county boroughs, but like professional attitudes, there are established inter-service differences which may be used. They may not operate uniformly across authorities, but the differences may be ignored at the rather general level of discussion being adopted here. Staff factors may affect the use of substitute services, and also the degree to which some services are neglected, though we shall only have the second kind of measure.

The area in which most information is available is of course finance. Here we are not concerned with central grants as such but rather with the independent financial capacity of particular local authorities. The extent of available resources and the willingness to use them are of interest. One immediate indicator of the first is the level of rate deficiency grant, which was calculated on the basis of local resources so as to equalise local income.(22) Without arguing the case for equalisation (23) this grant clearly acknowledges the variation of local resources, and attempts to measure them in concrete terms.

Of more direct interest for our purposes are the local tax base and the decisions about its exploitation. Ignoring their revenue from other sources local authorities behave very differently towards their ratepayers. This clearly affects their spending power. The rate to be levied seems very inelastic within any authority and the factors which explain that inelasticity are most important. A very low and inelastic rate level is a major limitation on local financial resources. The rateable value will be taken as indicative of potential resources, and the rate as indicative of the willingness to tax. It is assumed that this willingness is affected by the prevailing level of rate, and also by certain features of the rate base. In this sense, as has been observed, the rate is like any other service and will be treated as such below. Ultimately, of course, the level of resources is a combination of base and exploitation, which may be measured by the rate call or, more accurately, by the rate call controlled for population size.

These then are the major indicators of a fairly general kind which relate to our conceptual scheme. Some of them are crude and others very precise, but in combination they will permit us to apply the scheme to a

34

range of services to check its relevance and its potential. In our existing state of knowledge any development is important and even unsophisticated measures are useful, particularly as they point to areas where more detailed material may be collected.

4 The Services

The remainder of this work will be taken up with applying the theoretical
scheme just outlined to a range of services provided by English and Welsh
county boroughs. This will serve as a test of the explanatory potential of
the scheme and will demonstrate the importance of different characteristics
of county boroughs in explaining policies. The reasons for choosing county
boroughs have already been elaborated, but there is no reason why the
scheme should not be applied at other levels of the local government
system. (1)

With the county borough as setting a variety of dependent variables
might have been studied. One might have taken a particular issue or decision, or a number of such decisions in some issue area. The earlier refer-
ences to the literature on community politics, however, indicated that our
interests were wider than this, and the operational indicators outlined in
Chapter 3 are relevant to a different level of analysis. Robert Alford in the
essay already quoted distinguishes three levels of dependent variable. (2)
In increasing order of generality they are the decision, the policy and the
role of government. The first may be explained by particular situational
factors but is in part determined by the outcomes at a higher policy level.
Many decisions are pre-empted by a declared policy position. The latter,
like the role of government, is explained by more permanent structural and
cultural characteristics of each local area. Our concern is with policy,
though it has incidental relevance for the role of government. Thus while
it is important to understand the determinants of housing and welfare
policy, it is also important to isolate factors relevant to the overall level of
government action within which these particular services have to be seen.
Having reviewed some of the major independent variables to be applied in
the study, it remains to look at the service areas, and at the operational
measures of services which will be used.

It has not been possible to review the whole range of local activity
which is very extensive. Measures of some activities are extremely difficult to obtain, and much of the most important work of local authorities is
internal to the governmental structure. The Clerk's and Treasurer's
Departments are the most obvious examples of significant 'services' for
which external measures are almost impossible to find. This is equally
true for other departments such as Architects' and Planning, despite their
very high significance for important programmes such as urban renewal.
The impact of such departments is mediated through others, such as housing, education, highways and parks. The quality of the environment, or the
speed of development may be a direct function of the Planners' work, but
their impact is more understandable in terms of house completions and
demolitions, areas of open space and municipal amenities, which are run by
other departments.

The result is that attention will be focused on eight services: education, children, health, welfare, libraries, police, fire and housing, where the outputs have direct public relevance. This leaves out a number of important services such as highways, parks, refuse disposal and sewerage. It does, however, provide a range of services which vary widely in important respects, and will thus provide an adequate test for the proposed model. At the same time, these services account for seventy per cent of total local government spending, with the result that they collectively dominate the overall role or scope of government. The chosen services also seem likely to throw some light on traditional interests. They relate to various central departments and operate under widely different legislative authority. They have been part of the local government sector for varying lengths of time and have enjoyed different periods of development. In short, it is claimed that they give a good coverage of local activity.

For each of these services consideration was given to the choice of appropriate measures of activity. Gross expenditure was examined first as indicating the total effort applied to a particular service. As in various other studies this was found to vary very closely with population size. This very high and expected association offered problems of analysis and one has to agree with Wood's comment that 'Community Size is so faithful a bedfellow to public spending that one of our aims must be to lift it out of the way - hold it constant, so to speak - in order to measure whatever other factors are underneath.'(3) While this fact may justify some of the traditional concern with size it does not help us to locate other factors which may give rise to varied activity.

Accordingly, for each service except housing, the principal measure being used will be the annual expenditure per thousand population met from rate and grant sources, giving some control over the major effect of size. Such a measure, if it is to be treated as a measure of service provided, demands some explanatory comment, as it is often considered inadequate for a variety of reasons. It is inevitable that variation in expenditure will not directly relate to variations in the quality of service provided. Nevertheless, we would go a long way with Wildavsky in arguing that,

'Taken as a whole the ... budget is a representation in monetary terms of governmental activity. If politics is regarded in part as conflict over whose preferences shall prevail in the determination of national policy, then the budget records the outcome of the struggle. If one asks, "Who gets what the government has to give?" then the answers for a moment in time are recorded in the budget. If one looks at politics as a process by which government mobilises resources to meet pressing problems then the budget is a focus of their efforts.'(4)

Thus we shall be analysing resource allocations to various services in all county boroughs, though with the implicit assumption that these allocations do tell us something about the quality of service intended, and about the level of service provided.

Personal experience in various authorities suggests that this is a reasonable general claim, and some of our data gives added point. Several indicators aimed at reflecting the kind of service provided were correlated with levels of expenditure, with the results shown in Table 4-1. The size of these correlations justifies the claim that expenditure and service are closely related in these areas and evidence from other studies also bears out the reasonable nature of the claim. (5) Bleddyn Davies in a study of aspects of three local services has admirably summarised the problems of using expenditure measures, because 'prices of commodities vary between areas ... local authorities may differ greatly with respect to the efficiency with which they spend their money ... income and expenditure data ... is not everywhere collected in a manner ... strictly comparable', and so on. (6) He allows, however, that local accounts have become more satis-factory, and that 'in certain circumstances (they) form the most compre-hensive index available, since higher expenditures generally imply higher standards.'(7) Thus while admittedly we are using a crude index this seems justified in a field where the level of knowledge is low and where even broad relationships are unexplored. There is a danger, too, that in taking any more detailed measures (though some which follow are less general) one is approaching closer to the level of particular decisions. Certainly such details can result from more particular considerations than those which give rise to policy decisions. To the extent that this is true, the explanation for such outcomes needs to be sought among factors other than the general community-wide ones being examined here.

Among the more detailed policy outcomes which might be considered some have already been introduced. Comprehensive school development is one such and council house sales would be a somewhat parallel case, though the centrally imposed limitation prevents analysis of this. Crime detection rates and numbers of policemen might also be considered, together with numbers of books in library stocks. These and other measures will be elaborated where relevant in particular sections and will serve to qualify the expenditure measures. In the area of council housing the main depen-dent variable will be the proportion of new local houses provided by the local authority, as expenditures are less easy to compare in this field.

The eight chosen services vary in a number of interesting and valuable ways, as was noted earlier. To give more clarity to such variations the services may be arranged in relation to the various dimensions of needs, dispositions and resources which have been discussed. Essentially these services are being conceived as fulfilling needs, using resources and re-flecting dispositions, and arranging them in this context greatly facilitates

Table 4-1. Simple correlations between selected measures of service and spending

Library	Book stock per capita	0.638
Fire	Rateable value of property/firemen	−0.625
Police	Number of population/policemen	−0.814

subsequent analysis by indicating explicit hypotheses very clearly. Looking at needs first, services have to be arranged in terms of both scope and basis of need, though viewed from the providing and not the receiving end. There is always the problem in this context of distinguishing between the availability of a service and its actual use. Thus while public libraries are universally available in county boroughs, they tend to be used by only certain sections of the community.

Services may vary in two ways. They may vary in their incidence, and here we are concerned simply with objective incidence. Some will cater for the whole community while others cater for a distinguishable section of the community. They will also vary in their 'packageability' or in the degree of precision with which they may be directed. (8) There are services, like museums, which cannot easily be directed even within the limits of the one community, though attempts are often made to benefit locals in their use of such provision. At the same time, there are health services and some cultural provisions which are aimed at some section of the community but are available to all. These two distinctions give the following possible service positions:

| | Services which | |
Services which	May be precisely directed	May not be precisely directed
Are broad in scope	1	2
Are narrow in scope	3	4

It is at once fairly obvious that categories 2 and 3 are likely to provide most of the cases. Extensive services are unlikely to be easily directed and less extensive services are. This distinction produces two broad sets of services. The first set cater for the whole community in intention if not in practice. They have to be provided on a community-wide basis, though they may not be consumed equally widely. The second set cater more precisely for some narrower range of consumers. These services are listed below. This is not intended to imply that all services do not have general

Set one		Set two
Fire	Museums	Welfare
Police	Art galleries	Children
Libraries	Theatres	Housing
	Transport	Education
	Roads	Personal health
	Public health	

benefits for the community, but simply that in our second category these will be incidental. Nor is it intended to imply that decisions about the first group ignore the more likely beneficiaries of the service. This may be an important factor in establishing dispositions and will be considered in the detailed analysis.

Turning to the basis of need as relating to the physical-personal dimension, placement of services is somewhat easier, though care needs to be taken with cases where joint influences occur. Though it is not absolutely accurate it is reasonable to assume that physical needs are met by physical provision which appears in the budget as capital spending. In the same way, personal services are likely to involve high labour content and this will be reflected in revenue spending in the budget. Allowing that the categories are not completely self-contained, Diagram 4-1 shows the proportion of revenue to capital spending on various services over a six-year period. Some modification may be necessary, where physical provision or capital spending is a substitute for more direct personal provision, but the overall picture is clear.

The graph shows two important features. In the first place it shows quite clearly the tendency for the predominantly revenue spenders to alter the balance of their spending in favour of capital account over time. In spite of this it also reveals three quite distinct groups of services which vary widely in their revenue-capital ratios.

Diagram 4-1 Ratio of revenue to capital spending on ten selected local services for all Local Authorities, 1960-6

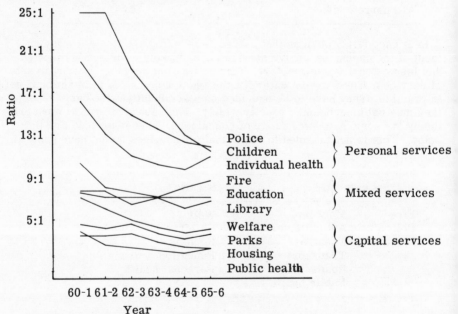

The increased capitalisation of three services seems to have a reasonably straightforward explanation. The police service has undergone a major technical revolution in recent years. This has involved the use of more refined equipment and the development of much more mechanised forces. At the same time antiquated police buildings are likely to have been replaced. In the case of the children's service it seems likely that residential care of a long-term and short-term variety has been developed. Also the early 1960s may mark a period of new building for such purposes, with heavy capitalisation involved. The individual health services may be explained by similar factors, though the transition is less abrupt and therefore less difficult to understand.

In spite of these changes over time the three services stand out as the most personal, as one would expect in the case of children and individual health. The extensive labour element in the police service, however, while not altogether surprising, may be very important, particularly as there is an acute shortage of recruits. It may in fact account for some of the increased use of capital resources in the 1960s, partly designed as a substitute for scarce labour resources.

The other two groups offer few surprises, parks and public health being added to our chosen services to indicate other highly capitalised services. Only the placement of welfare demands much comment, particularly as it shows a consistently low ratio over the whole period. One assumes that the explanation lies in the incidence of old people's homes, facilities for day care and for the handicapped, coupled with the fact that the labour component is invariably quite low. (9) It does, however, mark off the service from children and individual health which would at first sight appear very similar. Again it may be the labour problem as much as the pattern of need which creates this ratio of spending, but it has important repercussions. Policy decisions in highly capitalised services impose different pressures from those in which labour content is much heavier. The latter involve resources which are often scarce as well as an obvious pressure for recurrent expenditure.

This introduces the resources element in our model and the diagram has direct relevance for the use of labour. Treating the high revenue spenders as heavy labour users (with the exception of housing where interest charges are so important), it becomes clear which services are likely to be exposed to any labour shortages. This tends to be compounded by other problems concerned with alternative employment opportunities and the overall availability of trained personnel. As in the case of the police, so in other services, it may lead to the development of labour substitutes or to a shortfall in the level of service provided.

Whatever the labour position, the major resource involved in most services is finance. This is why it is appropriate to treat money allocations as the major dependent variable. The relative cost of the services selected is shown in Diagram 4-2. This indicates the extent to which they collectively dominate local expenditure and the contribution which each of the services makes to the overall total. Education and housing occupy dominant positions, both generally and in the context of our limited selection. They also dominate on both revenue and capital account, though our major concern is with the former.

41

Diagram 4-2 Proportion of capital and revenue spending devoted to each of the chosen services by Local Authorities.

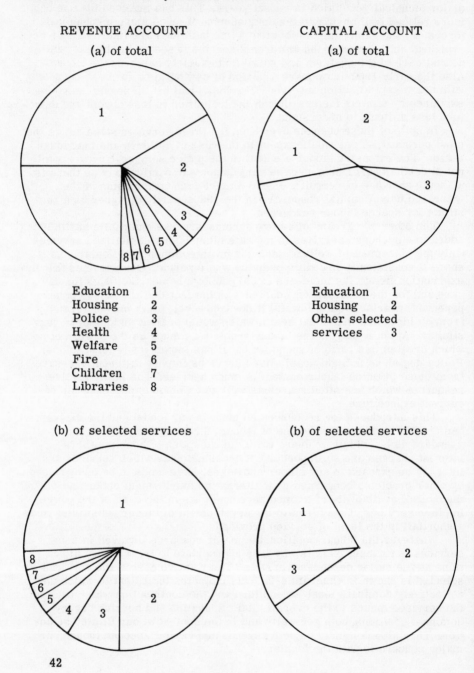

REVENUE ACCOUNT

(a) of total

CAPITAL ACCOUNT

(a) of total

Education	1
Housing	2
Police	3
Health	4
Welfare	5
Fire	6
Children	7
Libraries	8

Education	1
Housing	2
Other selected services	3

(b) of selected services

(b) of selected services

While this presentation illustrates the overall impact of each service, it must be considered in association with some appraisal of the elasticity of such spending. Periodic central government requests for economies in local spending bring this problem into sharp focus. At first sight it would appear that the most expensive services could be pruned most easily, but this does not appear to be the case. For national and local reasons such services have strongly established positions and are difficult to alter. The very scale of their spending is probably indicative of their strength in acquiring funds.

Finally, much the most difficult of our dimensions is that of disposition. The comments already made give some indication of how individuals may react to different services. Scope and scale are obviously two important factors which influence dispositions about services. At the same time, it is possible to place services, even if only roughly, in relation to the broad dimensions of disposition.

In the first place, services will vary in the degree to which standards of provision may be determined, with obvious implications in terms of need. Acute under-provision would be obvious for most services, but national minima tend to prevent this becoming relevant. Above such minima, evaluation of physical provision would appear more straightforward than evaluation of personal services. This may account for a traditional focus, in many authorities, on house building rather than housing management. This is true whether one is considering the quantity or the quality of provision. Measurement of service output is notoriously difficult, but more particularly so in some of the personal services. Measurement of quality is often a matter of personal taste and is probably equally difficult in any service.

In terms of the areas to which services are directed the broad distinctions are clear. The division of services on a community-wide or a particular basis will provide a major basis for orienting dispositions. Wherever there is a clear client group, and the service may be closely directed, disposition will have a clear group basis on which to operate. The major confusion arises from those services which are universally available, but not generally used. Here some ambivalence may be present among policy-makers, as is often the case with 'culture for the masses' campaigns.

Finally, dispositions towards the legitimacy of government provision will apply. Most simply this will relate to the global effort of the authority measured in financial terms. In addition attitudes may vary towards the levels adopted in particular services. Thus there are those who think that government spending has gone as far as it should, while recognising that the distribution of spending could usefully be modified. Provision of non-vocational education or of pre-school education might be questioned, as might the provision of council houses.

This review of services in terms of disposition has necessarily been rather vague. It is difficult to be precise about services at this general level and observers may be ambivalent towards different aspects of any one service. Before moving to the analysis of particular services it may be worth considering the likely relevance of different services to the public, councillors and officials.

43

For the public the overwhelming fact is the generally low salience of local government activity. Detailed comments will be made on particular services, but the overall impression is one of low involvement and little awareness. Survey evidence shows two important findings. In terms of electors' knowledge of the local government system, evidence prompts the comment: 'There seems to be a certain level of general public ignorance concerning local government and the services provided by the council.'(10) On the related question of contact, the same survey reported that 'Almost everyone has some "contact" with the council...', (11) but this had to be severely qualified. Only twenty-six per cent had had some contact with the town hall or council office in the last year and only six per cent had contacted a councillor in the last year. Taken together with low turn-out at local elections these figures suggest that public disposition may not be very important. Or it may only be important as mediated through voluntary groups or 'anticipated reactions' of councillors and officers.

In terms of councillors one of the most important general observations is the low salience of parties. This view, which this work is designed to test, springs not only from the attitude towards central control. It stems from a more fundamental view of local government as an administrative device. Comprehensive schools, council rents and direct labour services are the only areas of party difference normally cited. Party is additionally considered in relation to local patronage, (12) but not as it relates to policies.(13) This work tests the assumption that party is relevant and that the parties divide along the lines indicated in Chapter 3. Party affiliation will be treated as a reliable guide to councillor disposition.

Finally, in terms of the bureaucracy it is more difficult to be precise. Local action is clearly very relevant to them, but there is no convenient party shorthand for summarising their attitudes. While it may be assumed that most officials share a general commitment to government action, their impact in different services will be varied. It is possible that those services with the longest history of development have become much more professionalised, with increased potential for official influence. In the same way, some services are provided by more established professionals and this affects their impact. Finally, the sheer size of the professional staff has an important bearing on this question.

Other interpretations are possible with these sorts of development. Long-established departments may find their professional staffs developing accommodations with political realities of which they are more aware. Newly professionalised services may have more developed skills than those of longer standing. Data on many of these issues are not readily available and our detailed analysis will adopt the earlier set of assumptions equating older departments with greater professionalism. Detailed comments on the particular services will be made in the individual analyses.

5 Education

Among the many services provided by local authorities, education is perhaps the most important. Certainly in terms of resources devoted to the
service it is outstanding, both in terms of capital and revenue account. (1)
This financial significance shows no sign of diminishing, and the recent trend
has been towards an increase. The increasing expectations of parents for
their children, and of educationists and politicians generally, seem likely to
maintain this growth into the future as well, though other pressures are very
apparent. This is not different in principle from the position in other services but is more significant in an area where the level of expenditure is
already somewhat disproportionately high. The significance of education,
however, goes far beyond its financial implications. The full utilisation of
our individual talent and the collective development of many aspects of
our national life depend in large measure on the quantity and quality of the
education provided by local authorities. It is this fact which lies at the core
of pressures to centralise and create uniform standards and which has
given rise to the numerous reforming reports on the educational system. (2)
That many of the recommendations in such reports are not implemented
reflects in part the existing financial pressures and the cost implications
of the reforms.

In spite of this widely accepted view of the importance of education,
and in spite of a legislative framework which gives the Secretary of State
a close controlling role, (3) the variety of educational provision among local
authorities remains substantial, as we have shown in Chapter 2. The range
of per capita expenditure is very wide, and in one particular policy area,
that of secondary reorganisation, the local authorities reveal dramatic differences. The figures for 1967 reveal that more than half of the county
boroughs had no thirteen-year-olds in such schools and the range among the
remainder was from 95.0 per cent to 0.1 per cent. This variation was accentuated by the rather polarised distribution among these county boroughs.
Similar variation may also be seen in other aspects of the educational
system, and is most overtly recognised in the designation of educational
priority areas by the Department of Education. This policy acknowledges
the relative inadequacy of certain areas within certain authorities, and by
so doing suggests obvious differences between authorities in terms of the
problems faced, or in terms of the techniques used to deal with them, or
both. Areas within authorities vary, but by implication, so do authorities.

A tacit acceptance of this variation seemed to underlie a recent comment in 'The Times' (4) on departmental statistics, showing details of local
provision. This pointed out the wide variation between authorities, though it
was content to attribute the variation to 'luck'. It is not important here to
argue whether 'The Times' was right to label Solihull 'perhaps the most
privileged area educationally in England', on the basis of the percentage of

children attending grammar schools after the age of eleven. It is important, however, to ask why Solihull 'enjoys' this position, and to ask what it is about Solihull that contributes to this state of affairs. The report also commented on some authorities who, like Solihull, do consistently well in educational terms and some who do not. This very consistency suggests that there may be some equally consistent local features which explain these variations. The traditionalist who argues the strength of central control over local authorities has to explain this variation in terms of central decisions either to foster variety, or at least to permit it. The alternative explanation, which seems more probable, is that the centre cannot exercise such tight control over the localities in respect of some features of educational policy, and that consequently local factors have considerable impact on those policy areas.

The model of local policy-making which was outlined in Chapter 3 is designed to distinguish some of the local factors which may lead to such policy variations. It is not proposed as a comprehensive explanation of educational policy, as many important factors are both difficult to determine and still more difficult to operationalise and measure. It is, however, suggested as an explanation of a proportion of educational variation, and this is particularly so as we are concerned with the very broadest indicator of policy variation. It is in particular areas that one might expect less available indicators to be of relevance.

Thus it is most obvious that different education authorities are faced with different school populations, certainly in proportionate terms, and this must be a cardinal indicator of need. The number of children aged between five and fifteen does vary from place to place, and the compulsory nature of the educational service ensures that such differences will be translated into the policy process, at least in overall terms. The importance of such pressures was very apparent in the recent decision to postpone the raising of the school leaving age, which would have had a predictable and significant impact on local educational authorities. Equally salient for our more general point is the fact that some education authorities were obviously not able to meet the demands which the extra year would have imposed. This was accepted by central government and extra funds were allocated to local authorities to cope with their additional problems. But while the age structure of the population creates an obvious need, it is less obvious which other features will be so directly relevant in the overall sense. In addition to its broad age basis, the service provides for the bulk of the school-age population, thus cutting across a number of major lines of cleavage which might be important. As a result the social composition of an authority will have less effect on overall spending. It may have greater consequences for the direction in which funds are spent and this may have further financial repercussions. Especially is this the case where grammar school and sixth form places are much more costly than other forms of provision. Some kinds of school do cater disproportionately for some sections of the population and we will examine one of these later. The important point here is that the bulk of the education budget does not go on such schools and that the impact of this characteristic of the population may not, therefore, show in overall spending.

46

But these comments derive from viewing the education service as a personal one in terms of our earlier classification of the basis of need. In Chapter 4, however, the service appeared very clearly as a more mixed one, involving heavy capital expenditure. There is thus a distinct physical aspect to be considered, both in its own right but also as strongly reinforcing many of the more direct population pressures on the service. This dual impact is most obviously produced by the extent of physical school provision and its adequacy, and by the general condition of such facilties. The physical upheaval of urban-renewal programmes is one powerful factor in this connection. The pressure for new school buildings can be a major influence, particularly as there is usually no available alternative, however inadequate, where people are resettled. Even more obvious is the need created by crowded and dilapidated schools. The implications for school building are obvious, but there are innumerable related teaching and social problems which fall on the education authority. These may take the form of extended education welfare services, or of ancillary provision to create positive discrimination in favour of such schools. All of these are relevant but all are difficult to evaluate and to measure. Inevitably this makes them difficult to incorporate in our analysis and they will only receive passing attention. They would, however, merit detailed consideration elsewhere.

If needs are important, in any of the ways outlined, so too may disposition be important in an area where expenditure is heavy and issues often highly controversial. This is certainly true in party political terms, this being one of the few services in which party conflict is widely acknowledged. (5) It may be objected that the compulsory nature of the service reduces local autonomy and that this seriously dilutes party differences. However, the variation in expenditure which has been shown suggests that this is rather an hypothesis to be tested than an established fact. Certainly party appears to have influenced one major piece of educational policy-making in terms of secondary reorganisation. The government circular already referred to(6) allowed a good deal of discretion to local education authorities about both the timing and the content of their reorganisation plans. Party control has been shown to be a very relevant factor in determining local reactions in this field, at least in terms of the submission of plans.(7) In fact the whole notion of a partnership between central government and local authorities in education implies local autonomy around which party might be important.

Given this, one might expect political differences to show themselves in a number of ways. The scale of education spending and its impact on the overall scope of government suggest one basic difference. If our earlier point about Labour councils favouring government action is correct, then this should show in a greater commitment to a major service like education. They would be less interested in trimming the service to 'essentials'. This would be reinforced by other aspects of disposition. One might expect Labour councils to favour provision for the under-privileged sections of the community. In terms of need the source could become most significant in political terms, as is clear in the social arguments in favour of comprehensive schools. Not that all Labour authorities agree over how to help the disadvantaged, many favouring extended opportunities for grammar school entry.(8) Similar arguments could be extended to other aspects of education, including ancillaries like school meals and medical services. These latter are rather marginal to this expensive service, but commitment to the lower-class sector has substantial overall cost implications. In the broadest sense it would involve spending in those parts of the service which cater for the majority of the school-age population, elite segments being only small in numbers.

This party distinction may thus be very indicative of collective councillor dispositions. Official and public attitudes are less easily summarised. Available evidence suggests that public knowledge of this service is low, though this is true of most services. It also shows that very few people involve themselves with the service in terms of enquiries or complaints.(9) This could be construed as reflecting a lack of interest in this sphere of local government action, but other information opens up other possibilities. Educational items do not occupy very prominent news positions and popular attitudes may be a reflection of the complexity of the service or the opacity of policy and decision processes.(10) In any event it is more surprising in a sphere where very severe rate implications might have been expected to generalise interest beyond the direct consumers of the service.

This individual lack of information and involvement may itself account for the emergence in recent years of a number of organisations concerned with educational problems. They have been concerned both to mobilise the public more fully and to press for certain kinds of policy. The Confederation for the Advancement of State Education and the Advisory Centre for Education are two of the most firmly established. They do not seem to have been unduly successful but this probably reflects the very general nature of their aims. Organisations with more limited aims have been more successful. The Comprehensive Schools Committee, campaigning for that form of secondary school organisation, has been reasonably successful, though this may largely be due to the general tide of opinion flowing their way on that issue.

More interesting and important in general terms is the opposition to such reorganisation mounted in many localities, but most impressively in the London Borough of Enfield. A group of parents undertook a wide series of actions culminating in a High Court conflict with the Secretary of State for Education. Though they failed to prevent the move to comprehensives in the ultimate, their campaign illustrates a number of important features. Obviously this will be a rare form of activity and will require people with high skills and resources, both of which were available in this case. At the same time, they operate most successfully on issues where opinion is divided and where procedures are complicated and opportunities for action frequent. Above all, this case would demonstrate the greater ease of preventive or delaying action compared with any positive efforts which might be called for. Local authority innovation has not been the subject of close scrutiny, but the inertia and caution of local councils is often noted and probably makes external pressure for innovation very difficult.

The pattern of relationships between the variables which have been outlined and per capita spending on education is shown in Table 5-1. This shows only the simple relationships between the variables, but a number of features become clear at once. In very broad terms the table gives support to the relationship between spending and needs, dispositions and resources which has been suggested.

The most obvious relationship in the table, coinciding with our expectation, is that between spending and the school-age population taken as a measure of need. This probably reflects the significance of the school sector in the total education service and the fact that this is the compulsory aspect of local education. This can have important implications for other aspects of the service, as is now being shown in the application of economies by education authorities which are primarily affecting further education, especially the non-vocational sectors. The other general indicator of need, social class composition, also shows a close relationship with spending. This suggests that social composition may have a greater and more general impact than we had suggested. Again this is a relationship with most significant implications.

These implications are mainly related to the other features connected with this kind of social composition. The incidence of other needs is likely to be greater in lower-class authorities, as we shall see, but above all they seem certain to have less resources with which to meet their needs. This is confirmed by our indicators of local resources which show that it is the poor authorities who spend most, despite their relative poverty. The somewhat contradictory nature of this relationship, like that with class, has special importance because of the great cost of education. An authority can only spend within its global budget and what it spends on education cannot go on other services. Central contributions obviously help poor authorities to discharge their heavy obligations, but still education decisions will have repercussions on other services. The relative significance of central finance will be taken up later.

Before looking more closely at the relationships just outlined, the strong correlation between disposition and spending must be emphasised. Labour councils do spend more than Conservative councils, indicating a much wider relationship between party and education than is usually observed. It is usually accepted that party control is related to specific educational questions like comprehensivisation, but not to the overall level of activity of the education authority. This narrower view of the relevance of party is probably a product of the tendency to focus on areas of public controversy and cleavage, effectively excluding much of the educational service. The relationship shown here indicates the significance of party control, which is ignored in most writing on the subject. While education may have a very professional element it is also related to party influence, reflecting the divergent values of the two parties.

Though it is not easy to take them into account, the table shows several relationships aimed at reflecting the impact of the bureaucracy and of the public. The significance of need would seem to imply an elaborate role for officers because of their technical preoccupation with such legal factors. The same would be true of the fact that education seems to flourish even where resources are scarce. If local authority departments do compete for resources, and this is most likely in the poorest areas, then education seems to do well, reflecting high performance by its officials as well as the parties.

Table 5-1. Simple correlations between per capita Education spending and
selected indicators of need, disposition and resources

Indicator	Correlation
NEED	
Total population	0.074
Per cent of population aged 5-14	0.630
Per cent of population in social classes I & II	—0.462
Per cent of population in social classes IV & V	0.420
DISPOSITION	
Councillors	
Per cent Labour membership on the council	0.522
Public	
Per cent turn-out in local elections 1964	—0.038
Per cent turn-out in local elections 1965	—0.201
Officials	
Number of committees	0.069
Number of sub-committees	—0.080
Employment of an O and M officer	—0.047
RESOURCES	
Rate levied	0.493
Per capita rateable value	—0.269
Level of rate deficiency grant	0.319

However acceptable at the intuitive level, these features are not reflected in the figures used in Table 5-1. Several indicators of officer autonomy fail to show any marked relationship. While this may invalidate the
point just made, it should be interpreted cautiously as the figures are for
the authority as a whole and not just for education. Thus to the extent that
they imply bureaucratic influence, they do so for all departments alike. This
means that the true impact of education officials may be lost in a combined
figure reflecting the varied degree of official competence in different departments.

The same is true of the voting turn-out figures used to indicate public
involvement. They probably reflect overall and rather unspecific tendencies
which may only incidentally affect education. In any event they show only a
very low order of relationship which is not surprising given many previous
findings on public awareness of, and interest in, services generally. More
precise indicators of group mobilisation and activity might of course reveal
relationships with spending, but they are difficult to acquire on a reliable
basis.

These simple correlations, however, reflect relationships which call for much closer examination. The relationship with party may be no more than a product of the fact that Labour councils tend to control working class districts, and class may be the operative factor. Equally, the relationship between class composition and age structure raises the question of whether spending responds to class pressures or is really a result of the numerical pressure of a given school-age population. In the same way, lack of local resources is itself related to low social class composition with consequent problems in interpreting the relationship with local resources. These interrelationships are examined more fully in Tables 5-2 and 5-3 which show

Table 5-2. Partial correlations between per capita Education spending and selected indicators of need, disposition and resources

| Effect of | Controlling for | | | | | |
	Age 5-14	Class IV & V	Labour	Rate	Grant	Value
Age 5-14	0.630	0.518	0.481	0.625	0.580	0.592
Class IV & V	0.024	0.420	0.084	0.324	0.310	0.339
Labour	0.271	0.351	0.522	0.390	0.450	0.466
Rate	0.484	0.421	0.343	0.493	0.419	0.437
Grant	0.111	0.118	0.123	0.147	0.319	0.181
Value	0.031	—0.056	—0.048	—0.092	—0.030	—0.269

Table 5-3. Partial correlations between per capita Education spending and selected indicators of need, disposition and resources

| Effect of | Controlling for | | | | | |
	Age 5-14 & Class IV & V	Age 5-14 & Labour	Age 5-14 & Grant	Class IV & V & Labour	Class IV & V & Grant	Labour & Grant
Age 5-14				0.495	0.517	0.470
Class IV & V		—0.156	—0.025			0.041
Labour	0.309		0.251		0.345	
Grant	0.111	0.037		0.099		

partial correlations between the main variables involved. These indicate the degree to which any one of our factors retains its relationship with educational spending independently of each of the others.

These partial correlations immediately answer a number of the questions just raised. Most obvious, but most significant, is the fact of need. Given a population structure in which the younger age groups are represented disproportionately, there will be greater spending on schools. This will apply whatever the class composition, party structure or level of resources in the area - that is, whatever the dispositions and resources. This seems to be a product of the compulsory nature of the service which automatically converts the needs of the locality into effective demands for educational spending. While this is relatively obvious it raises a number of questions in an acute form. If the effect of need is felt irrespective of local resource levels, what are the implications for other services of the resultant shortage of resources? What variation might one expect in those areas of the education service which are non-compulsory (was it this factor which directed local attention to those aspects when cuts were called for)? Whatever the answers to such questions, the nature of the legislation appears to restrict local decisional autonomy to a degree. Though these are reasonably obvious facets of the education service, their implications for other services are significant. No other service is so clearly obligatory, and certainly none is as expensive, creating obvious scope for local initiatives.

From the tables it appears that the other indicator of need, class composition, does not exercise an independent effect. Its independent effect when local resources are controlled suggests that it may then be reflecting age structure or party control, both of which are closely related to class composition. This lack of independent effect would reflect our earlier expectation and confirms the fact that state school provision extends across class boundaries, particularly when the primary sector is included. Thus it seems that class has little effect on the total level of educational spending, though we shall later have call to look more closely at its particular effects.

Need, then, is the most obvious factor related to educational spending. In keeping with our model, however, and in spite of its compulsion, it does not operate alone. Disposition, conceived in party terms, is also related although the relationship is not so strong. Labour councils spend more whatever the context of need in which they find themselves, confirming their general orientation to government activity and to education in particular.

Finally, what do the tables tell us about the effect of local resources on this most expensive service? Using the level of rate deficiency grant as indicative of local resources, it is clear that this factor has little independent effect on the level of educational spending. Where need is present it will have to be met and resources must be found. Similarly, Labour councils, being disposed to spend on schools, are willing to find resources whatever their financial standing. This confirms the serious implications of this service for the pattern of service provided in other areas. It does not invalidate the resource element in our model but makes it more relevant in the wider context of the overall pattern of services. One would expect resources to impinge more directly on other services.

Thus we have a service in which needs and disposition produce a pressure for provision with resources automatically being channelled for this purpose. This suggests that finance may well be less salient to the setting of policies in this field despite its very considerable expense. Many decisions will in any case have only a marginal effect on the overall budget, unlike services where the same scale of item might have dramatic effect.

Two problems might now be raised. One concerns the relative efficiency with which funds are spent, though it has already been suggested that overall spending may be taken as a broad assessment of policy, allowing for variation in efficiency. In any event this is a difficult question which raises complex problems of educational values beyond the scope of the present enquiry. The other question is more amenable to discussion here and is concerned with the way in which educational spending is directed. Some aspects of spending are fairly directly controlled from outside, as has already been observed, but others might be considered. One important condition is that they must be rather broad policy matters if they are to be amenable to analysis with the kinds of variables being used here.(11)

One such area, though it is now becoming obscured by the move towards comprehensive schools, is the relative development of grammar schools in different localities. This was one of the areas of 'luck' referred to in 'The Times' article cited earlier, a comment which indicates the observable diversity of provision and the fact that this is seen by some as a qualitative indicator of educational provision.(12) Taking the year 1965-6 as the observation period, which avoids the complication of increased comprehensivisation, the variation in percentage of grammar school places was from almost forty per cent to between twelve and thirteen per cent. Given the permanent implications of their secondary education for most people's lives and the low level of later transfer to equivalent academic opportunities, this is a substantial difference and reveals an area of great local significance.

Once again, as with overall spending, one would expect a relationship between this figure and the age structure, though it may be the reverse of the earlier relationship. Grammar schools, even where most developed, never cater for even half of the secondary school population, and might depend for their development on the general impact of the remainder of the school system. Where there are large numbers of children to be catered for the grammar segment may be neglected somewhat. But whatever the overall implication of age structure it seems reasonable to assume that the class composition will be relevant in this case and constitute a clear need. Analysis of grammar school intakes reveals the high degree to which they recruit from the middle class. Thus, given the basis of the current selection procedures and the broad wishes of parents from different classes, it is reasonable to expect that a larger middle class population will create a need for more grammar schools.

Disposition on this factor also seems likely to be the reverse of that for education generally. Comment has already been made on the ambivalence displayed within the Labour Party towards grammar schools.(13) In spite of this, one would expect Labour councils to be less favourably disposed than Conservative ones, indeed some of the Labour spur towards comprehensive schools arises out of the differential grammar school provision which we are discussing. In fact much of the divergence of Labour view at the local level may relate only to certain areas in which the grammar schools have been developed by the Labour council, with a consequent attachment to them and a wish to see them preserved. These are likely to be special cases, however, and one expects to find that Labour councils have developed the modern and technical schools more fully.

In terms of resources, one would not expect grammar provision to depend on the level of local resources. However large the provision of grammar school places, they form only a small part of total spending. It may be that priorities within the overall pattern of education are significant, especially when cuts or extensions are being proposed, but for normal purposes this is less significant. Even if resources are not relevant, however, it seems likely that wealthy authorities will be more likely to have more grammar school places because of the relation between the needs factors already discussed and the bases of local wealth.

As in the more general case, Table 5-4 shows the simple relationships between these selected variables and the number of grammar school places. Before commenting on these, one other important point demands comment. This is the inverse relationship between the general educational spending and grammar school provision ($r -0.148$). Those factors related to high overall spending are inversely related to grammar provision, with the exception of the level of resources. This is possibly explained by the point, mentioned earlier, that pressures for basic spending allow few resources for use in special areas of narrow provision. More alarmingly, it indicates that those authorities who spend relatively little on education devote more of that spending to their grammar schools (assuming that more places do cost more to provide). The implications of this for secondary modern schools in such localities may be worth investigating. This relationship is somewhat akin to the recent case in which the government has diverted additional resources to selected areas within various local authorities, raising a number of questions about the previous allocations made by the local authorities themselves. In the same way that certain geographical subareas may be receiving disproportionately low allocations, so also may certain sections of the population, though the two are closely related in many cases.

Turning to the relationships in the table, they generally confirm the expectations just outlined. High social class composition and the presence of a low Labour percentage on the council do coincide with higher provision of grammar school places. There is also the expected inverse relationship with the size of the school-age population, and the lowest order of relationship is with the index of local resources, though surprisingly the poorer authorities show a positive relation with grammar school provision. This is the most problematic of the relationships, particularly as it conflicts in direction with that for social class composition, which would normally be inversely related to it. The explanation for this position may lie in the very low order of the relationship, but in any event should be clarified by the use of the partialling technique adopted in the earlier case. This will also serve

54

Table 5-4. Simple correlations between per cent of thirteen-year-olds in Grammar Schools and selected indicators of need, disposition and resources

Indicator	Correlation
NEED	
Population size	−0.119
Per cent of population aged 5-14	−0.254
Per cent of population in social classes I & II	0.302
Per cent of population in social classes IV & V	−0.212
DISPOSITION	
Councillors	
Per cent Labour membership on council	−0.180
Public	
Per cent turn-out in local elections 1964	0.310
Per cent turn-out in local elections 1965	0.254
Officials	
Number of committees	0.310
Number of sub-committees	0.077
Employment of an O and M officer	0.105
RESOURCES	
Rate levied	0.153
Level of rate deficiency grant	0.106
Per cent of rateable value high domestic properties	0.196

as a check on the independence of the other relationships which is again confused by the interrelation among the independent variables.

Again, as in the general case, our measures of officer impact show virtually no relationship. This is not very surprising as this case is even more specific than the earlier one, with the indicators less valuable as a result. While this need not necessarily mean that officers are unimportant, it renders the question somewhat academic here.

The indicators of public disposition are more closely related and may repay further investigation. Electoral turn-out, though a feature related to social class, shows a relationship with grammar school places. The literature on electoral behaviour suggests that causal relationships between turn-out and policy may be difficult to establish, but here we have some prima facie evidence for such a relationship in one part of a service. It will be interesting to see whether this maintains its relationship when other variables are taken into account.

The partial correlations in Table 5-5 at once clarify the range of factors associated with this dependent variable. In the first place, the class factor maintains its association when the other variables are controlled. In particular when the negative factor of a large school population is withdrawn, class shows an even stronger relationship. This indicates the potential of a clear need in determining service levels where there are no strong competing needs to leave scope for disposition or resources to become influential. Obvious needs can be met without the problem of having to resolve competing priorities.

Table 5-5. Partial correlations between per cent of thirteen-year-olds in Grammar Schools and selected indicators of need, disposition and resources

| Effect of | Controlling for | | | | |
	Age 5-14	Class I & II	Labour	Grant	Turn-out 1965
Age 5-14	−0.254	−0.087	−0.189	−0.320	−0.198
Class I & II	0.190	0.302	0.262	0.388	0.221
Labour	−0.050	0.091	−0.180	−0.255	−0.097
Grant	0.226	0.275	0.206	0.106	0.115
Turn-out 1965	0.198	0.145	0.206	0.258	0.254

Disposition is more interesting here than it was in the earlier, more general case. Party does not show a very strong independent relationship with the number of grammar school places. However, it is invariably a negative correlation showing the Conservative preference for grammar school provision. Effectively, however, councillor disposition does not appear to be very prominent in this case. On the other hand, turn-out in local elections is consistently related to this dependent variable. This remains true when the other factors are controlled, though it is least marked where the control is for social class. No doubt this reflects the close relationship between class composition and electoral turn-out. While it is necessary to exercise care with this relationship, because turn-out is not a precise indicator of public disposition, it gives added support to the idea of public impact. If, as one would expect, electoral activity coincides with other activity in voluntary associations and the like, our findings would seem to be accurate. The actual influence process need not be electoral, of course, but examination of this more detailed problem is beyond the scope of our analysis.

Finally, resources show the opposite relationship to that which was hypothesised, though they were not given great emphasis in our analysis of a relatively cheap area of provision. The tables show that the poorer authorities provide more grammar school places, particularly when the other variables are controlled. This relationship is most difficult to interpret as it seems most unlikely that the lack of resources causes this activity. It will clearly not prevent such provision of grammar schools, but it is likely that some other factor is at work in this case.

This relationship of grammar school provision to a number of local factors is very important, though it relates to an educational form which is being superseded. This could make the question of comprehensivisation of much greater significance, partly because it is so important for the future of the educational system, and partly because it is such a clear-cut example of local policy-making. A detailed analysis will not be included here, however, as a number of case studies of the issue have been undertaken and a comparative study in some detail is now in preparation.(14) In addition, an analysis of submission of reorganisation plans has been done using the same analytical scheme as is being used here.(15)

The results of that study are probably worth summarising, however, as they give strong support to the general scheme. Submission of plans for secondary reorganisation was positively related to Labour Party control of the council. It was also related to the social composition of the local population, middle-class areas being less likely to submit plans, as one would expect. Resources showed little relation to submission, a product largely of the timing of the analysis (1966), which meant that this was a symbolic output for most local authorities. Activity on comprehensives is still not very apparent, as the recent Department of Education statistics show, and it may be that resources are very effective in terms of implementation of any plans.

Table 5-6. Partial correlations between per cent of thirteen-year-olds in Grammar Schools and selected indicators of need, disposition and resources

Effect of	Controlling for					
	Age 5-14 & Class I & II	Age 5-14 & Labour	Age 5-14 & Grant	Class I & II & Labour	Class I & II & Grant	Labour & Grant
Age 5-14				−0.099	−0.136	−0.237
Class I & II		0.210	0.267			0.309
Labour	0.105		−0.122		0.049	
Grant	0.293	0.250		0.265		

There is no reason to pursue this topic further here as this summary is adequate for our immediate purposes, though it is an issue which should be investigated more closely. It is sufficiently clear that the patterns of relationship are similar for each of our dependent measures of educational activity. Obviously the very broad indicators being used mean that the most general dependent variable shows the closest relationship, and this is our major concern. More detailed factors could operate on particular aspects of the education service, though even in those our variables show considerable relationships. Certain broad features of party control, or disposition, of population character or need, and, to a more limited degree, of resources, do have a bearing on the extent and the direction of local educational activity. This is most significant in its own right, and receives added importance from the fact that this is a most expensive service, and may well affect the capacity for doing other things.

6 Housing

Like education, housing is, by a number of criteria, a very important local service. In terms of expenditure, it is of immense significance on both revenue and capital account, though its rent basis gives it a different financial setting from other local authority services. It has also been a feature of local activity for a long time, beginning in some towns as early as the 1860s.(1) Throughout its long development it has aroused varying attitudes, but it is generally accepted as a major social service and as a major redistributive agency. Certainly housing has been one of man's main needs and in towns one of his main problems, creating a great deal of incidental social distress. This gives housing a much wider relevance than it might otherwise have, adequate provision creating many additional social benefits.

An additional complication, less relevant in the case of education, is the existence of a substantial private sector in housing. Few people advocate total public provision. It remains true, however, that some people are unable to buy their own homes and the privately rented sector has often been inadequate both in scale and quality. More recently this has led to legislation to control this sphere, making the letting of property less attractive to many investors. This has reduced private sector provision still further and is not yet compensated by the emergence of housing associations to help buyers. Altogether this implies an extensive, and increasing, task for local housing authorities.

For all of these reasons the pattern of local housing activity and its underlying policies are most significant. Central government does exercise certain powers in the sphere of housing, but it is our claim that local factors and their implications are most important. This local autonomy is emphasised in the sphere of council house rents by a recent Prices and Incomes Board report(2) which stressed that in practice the system 'gives local housing authorities wide powers to set rents as they please'. If this is true for rents it seems no less likely to be true of a number of other related housing policies. The sale of council houses was one such case, though central limits placed on this do indicate the existence of central power which can be used when the circumstances are right.

As was mentioned briefly in Chapter 4, measuring of housing policy is more difficult than in other services. The use of a per capita spending measure would be obscured by the very different nature of housing finance. The long-term nature of housing costs and the importance of rent income are only two of the difficulties. Some alternative measures are not easy to obtain. These would include measures of housing management practice, or qualitative indicators of the housing stock. As a result, a more restricted choice has been made, but one which it is argued gives a close indication of the general attitude of the local authority towards council housing. Two aspects of local housing will be considered. The first is the relation of public to private house building in the post-war years. This will be measured as the percentage of all houses built in each area after the war which were built by the local council. While this does not take account of the absolute volume of building, it does indicate the relative degree to which local authorities responded to their local situations. (3) The second measure is the level of rate subsidy paid into the housing account by the authority. That is the amount which the council decide that the general population should pay towards the housing cost of those living in public housing. The crucial importance of this measure was apparent in the Prices and Incomes Board Report which noted that 'the essence of the problem of rents is the balance between rates and rents'. (4) In somewhat simplified terms the rate subsidy measures the willingness of the authority to redistribute resources from the owners of property to council tenants, though the latter also pay rates.

These two measures are a guide both to the action of the local council and to its attitudes towards tenants and ratepayers as two distinct sections of the community. Like our measures of educational spending, they may be analysed in terms of our explanatory scheme. Needs, dispositions and resources will relate to each of these broad policies. Need in particular would seem relatively clear. One would expect its scope to be narrow though the degree would vary with the area. As the Prices and Incomes Board observe, 'One of the primary purposes of local authority housing has always been the provision of low rent housing for lower income groups.'(5) While this has changed somewhat, a fact which they acknowledge, it is still sufficiently true to suggest the section of the population creating need. The incidence of low income families would create a most obvious need, at any rate in terms of the personal dimension which was established. Other personal factors might have a bearing on housing policy, but do not seem to have had. The age structure of the population could be important, though mainly for the type of housing rather than the volume. (6) Equally, one might today consider immigrants as a group with special housing needs, but there is no evidence of them being treated other than as poor groups. Often in fact they are treated less well than other groups, as in the case of residence qualifications to qualify for housing. (7)

Some of this may be due to a tendency among policy-makers to see housing in terms of its physical aspects rather than its personal. This is very obvious in the designation of unfit houses which is the responsibility of the Medical Officer in any case. It is equally clear in the tendency to concentrate on the scale of provision, often with little reference to quality or amenity. It is less clear when rents and subsidies are being considered, many observers thinking that these should relate to the tenant and not the property. In any event housing is a service likely to respond to both physical and personal needs.

Historically, local housing efforts were directed to the clearance of 'unfit' dwellings and the provision of better ones, invariably with public health as the major incentive to action. As well as being historically more important, physical factors are also more obvious to those taking policy decisions about housing. Physical criteria of housing standards, both in terms of building standards and occupation levels, are easier to establish than personal criteria relating to tenants. Being more obvious and more quantifiable, they are likely to have more impact on policy-making. This would apply particularly to house building, though this in itself has repercussions for the rents charged and the rate subsidy paid.

As measures of housing standards and provision, two variables will be used, though their precise interpretation is by no means unambiguous. (8) One such indicator is the availability of standard amenities in local houses. Where all of these are not present in a house this will be defined as indicative of a housing need, as it reflects the relative extent of inadequacy. It must be remembered here that local authority effort over the years reduces the level of such inadequacy and may render the indicator less valuable. Also it reflects a very low level of housing provision and would probably not satisfy some observers as genuinely reflecting inadequate housing. For our very broad purposes, however, it is probably adequate. The other measure is of crowding or the density of occupation per room. This tells us something about general social conditions but also about the adequacy of housing supply. The density above which one might regard the housing position as inadequate depends on personal judgement. Here the line has been drawn at one and a half persons per room, which does not seem a generous standard. (9)

One problem with both these indicators is that they do not reflect the geographical incidence of each of these problems within the authority. The same aggregate level of problem may be caused by very varied distributions on the ground, as is recognised when 'slum' conditions are acknowledged. A very heavy concentration of inadequate houses is a much greater problem than inadequate housing scattered more thinly. This may be an area in which larger authorities have greater problems. Concentrated problems are likely to be more apparent to policy-makers and at the same time more difficult to deal with. In spite of this our aggregate measures should give a guide to the relative existence of housing needs.

Needs are reasonably obvious in the housing field, but so too are certain aspects of disposition. Council housing, particularly at moderate rentals, is very much associated with the Labour Party. Housing policies, given the financial system with its lengthy borrowing and subsidy periods and the slowness of building, tend to be long-term. Regular control of the council would thus also seem to be important in this field. Our indicator of party control should account for both the directional and the permanent aspects of council housing policy. At the same time, one would expect Labour councils to operate rent levels more generous to tenants and consequently to pay higher rate subsidies. The direct association of the Labour Party with council tenants is obvious in local elections and among council tenants who sit on local councils.

Moving to the other two groups whose dispositions are important, it is more difficult to be precise. Housing is a service of vital significance to one sector of the population and they have mobilised on the subject quite often in recent years. Rent strikes are not uncommon and tenants' associations have appeared in many areas. Squatting has reappeared in the late 1960s as a manifestation of the continuing housing problem. In addition a number of organisations have appeared with housing as their major focus,

61

the principal one being Shelter. (10) Many of these factors point towards an important public disposition, though the Shelter organisation raises a number of interesting issues. It obviously heightens interest in the whole area of public housing and certainly acts as a pressure on government. At the same time it may have the effect of weakening pressure by its claims on behalf of its own activities. By acting as a substitute for government action, it does tend to undermine pressure for such action. One other point is that the primary emphasis of its pressure is on central government where important housing policy decisions are of course taken. This does mean, however, that its impact on local authority thinking and activity is less direct. Thus there is possibly some public effect in this area, but it is probably no greater than in the sphere of education.

The impact of local government officers on housing is also difficult to measure. The long-term nature of housing activity and the highly technical aspects of design and building suggest that officers will be influential. The scale and complexity of housing finance might reinforce this influence by making decisions more complex for laymen. One interesting possibility is the conflict which may occur between one set of professionals in the Treasurer's Department and other sets in housing management or design. Where such conflict exists it may reduce the impact of both sets of officers in relation to the political policy-makers. This could be reinforced where Direct Works Departments exist and are important in both house building and maintenance. They arouse such bitter political controversy that professional judgement is likely to be ignored for political purposes.

Before leaving the question of disposition, it should be noted that housing is a very different public activity from education. Whereas the latter engages very little public attention, housing is a very public activity. The research cited earlier (11) shows that this is the subject about which most people approach their councillors and local officers. It is also the area about which they had heard most recently in terms of local news coverage by the press. Such factors may not indicate greater direct public impact but they do suggest that this is a more sensitive area than education. This might produce a more cautious attitude among officers who are aware of the possible political repercussions of their actions. Such a view would tend to be reinforced by councillors who are heavily exposed to housing problems in the course of their council work. Both of these pressures should support party impact, in particular making action more likely where the party majority is most secure.

In terms of resources the position is more complex than in most services. Central contributions take the form of subsidies which have varied considerably in their intention over time. (12) This has meant that local decisions may reflect central wishes to some extent as they have financial incentives to do so. At the same time, the self-financing nature of providing houses for rent creates another sort of pressure on local financial resources. The choice of method of finance is central to our second dependent variable but our first has serious cost implications. One would expect such an expensive service to have severe resource implications, though these may be lessened by the importance of the rent element. In any event one would expect poorer authorities to experience greater need for a service of this kind and this would give a clear relationship with our resource indicators. Whatever else this implies, it does indicate the severe consequences which housing effort might have in reducing other areas of services.

Apart from financial resources, one other resource merits separate attention. Building materials and available labour are clearly significant, but more important still is the availability of land. This is particularly so in the long term when the inflexibility of local authority boundaries creates problems for many county boroughs. The Royal Commission on Local Government were very conscious of this resource problem when they observed 'the inability of the municipal authorities with the largest housing needs to find, within their own areas, the necessary land; in the general unwillingness of neighbouring planning authorities to allow them to build on land just beyond their boundaries'. (13) Two very relevant problems result from this situation. One concerns the difficult negotiations which have to be undertaken with neighbouring authorities to secure external land resources. The other is more relevant to our overall concern and involves the adoption of high-rise building to overcome the shortage of land. In the latter case costs become extremely high, but there are also serious social implications involved in that kind of development. (14)

The overall density of population will be taken as indicative of the availability of land. This can give only a rough guide as the actual land-use pattern will influence the density, industrial land reducing the density but not increasing the resources for housing development. It is our contention that this will only affect a number of extreme cases and that the more general relationship will operate.

Table 6-1 shows the relationships between these indicators of needs, dispositions and resources and the percentage of new housing built between 1945 and 1958 by the local authority. These correlations amply confirm the expectations of our model. The only exception to this is population size, which was included as possibly creating greater absolute and proportionate need. The absence of any relationship may mean that such expectations are ill-founded or that private housing effort is more possible and worthwhile in large cities. Certainly the market potential would support this view in the case of most larger towns.

This factor apart, the level of house building relates very closely to need measured in both personal and physical terms. Social class composition shows very close relationships with the level of building, as one expected. Age factors are related but examination of their relationships shows that they are subordinate to the class composition. As a result they have not been used in the analysis, though the correlations can be found in Appendix C. Physical factors show equally strong relationships, particularly in the case of household amenities. The size of the correlation coefficient for the density of occupation per room confirms the possible implications of a broad array of needs.

While needs are obviously important, disposition also shows a clear relationship, at least in terms of our indicator of party control. Labour-controlled councils show a distinct tendency to build more council houses than do their Conservative counterparts. This confirms the attitudes of the two parties to council housing as such and also to the desirable balance of

Table 6-1. Simple correlations between per cent of Local Housing
built by the council, 1945-58, and selected indicators of
need, disposition and resources

Indicator	Correlation
NEED	
Population size	0.028
Per cent in social classes I & II	−0.806
Per cent in social classes IV & V	0.652
Per cent of houses possessing standard amenities	−0.597
Number of persons per room	0.437
DISPOSITION	
Councillors	
Per cent Labour membership on council	0.670
Public	
Per cent turn-out in local elections 1964	−0.099
Per cent turn-out in local elections 1965	−0.099
Officials	
Number of committees	−0.103
Number of sub-committees	0.066
Employment of an O and M officer	0.142
RESOURCES	
Level of rate	0.430
Rate deficiency grant	0.464
Domestic rateable value	−0.695
Per capita rateable value	−0.398
Density of population	0.278

public and private action. The combination of these two elements in the one
policy area could account for the very substantial relationship.

As in the case of education, the measures designed to indicate public
and officer disposition do not show anything like such clear relationships.
The most that could be said on the basis of such figures would be that officer
autonomy is positively related to housing activity and public mobilisation
is not. The size of the relationships makes even these comments difficult
to examine and they will not receive more detailed treatment here. It must
be remembered, however, that they are the least adequate of our measures
and the question of public and official impact remains a very open one.

Finally, the table shows close relationships between building and each
of our resource indicators. Each of the financial indicators is closely re-

lated, as is the measure of land availability. The former relationships indicate the extensive financial implications of local housing activity. The latter suggests the relevance of this important resource. Care should be taken in interpreting this last relationship, however, as it is to some degree dependent on the level of council building which usually involves much higher densities. The figures do suggest, however, that land has not restricted local house building, though it may have affected many of its social consequences. Other causal factors may be generating housing activity and the densities created reflect the quality of such housing. In any event resources are involved, though not necessarily as direct causal factors.

Such ambiguities are difficult to sort out, and they are not the only ones left by the table. Party and social class are themselves related, making it impossible to tell whether each is exercising an independent effect. Equally class is related to the other need indicators and their independent effects on local authority building must be assessed, as either could be a spurious relationship. The partial correlations in Tables 6-2 and 6-3 attempt to sort out these complex interrelationships for our main indicators.

Table 6-2. Partial correlations between per cent of Local Housing built by the council, 1945-58, and selected indicators of need, disposition and resources

	Controlling for				
Effect of	Class IV & V	Crowding	Density of population	Labour	Grant
Class IV & V	0.652	0.563	0.620	0.3∧0	0.537
Crowding	0.198	0.437	0.354	0.269	0.365
Density of population	0.112	0.048	0.278	0.119	0.309
Grant	0.171	0.400	0.480	0.263	0.464

Note: Crowding = density of occupation per room.

These tables offer striking confirmation of the importance of needs, dispositions and resources for this service. Both the personal and the physical aspect of housing need maintain a strong effect independently of disposition and resources. They also operate independently of one another, though the personal indicator of social class composition has a much stronger relationship. This confirms the duality of the pressure for action in this field and may increase the likelihood of response to need. Either or both of these pressures may affect the awareness of policy-makers.

Table 6-3. Partial correlations between per cent of Local Housing built by the council, 1945-58, and selected indicators of need, disposition and resources

Effect of	Controlling for					
	Class IV & V & Crowding	Class IV & V & Labour	Class IV & V & Grant	Crowding & Labour	Crowding & Grant	Grant & Labour
Class IV & V				0.281	0.460	0.268
Crowding		0.184	0.193			0.245
Labour	0.384		0.384		0.541	
Grant	0.165	0.155		0.239		

Note: Crowding = density of occupation per room.

Perhaps politicians are affected by the personal and social implications of the housing situation, while officials react to the more precise objective criteria related to physical conditions.

These possible relationships between need and disposition are given some support by the considerable independent relationship between party control and building. Here indeed is an area where party is most relevant and where the declared positions of Labour politicians do result in action. In itself this is not particularly surprising, though the strength and consistency of the relationship are both impressive. Its importance lies in its wider implications. Here is confirmation of a Labour commitment to a second area of very costly provision. The implications of high spending on education and housing are serious for the remaining services. It will be recalled that together these services account for more than half of all local authority spending on both revenue and capital account. If party raises this proportion in an authority the results are obvious in terms of other services.

This is particularly the case when one also takes into account the impact of our measures of resources. The grant index of resources maintains an independent relationship with house building, confirming that poorer authorities are the major house builders. This is true when one controls for both need and disposition, which reinforces the comments above about the implications of high spending. Not only are certain major resource allocations likely in these authorities, but their implications are heightened by the relative poverty of such areas. Central grants may have an equalisation element but they cannot cope with pressures such as these.

The density of population factor is less regular in its relationships. It shows an independent relation in every case except when taken with the measure of crowding. This suggests that it might be better treated as a measure of need, which is a possible interpretation. It does not mean that land availability is not important but may reflect the housing difficulties which this particular indicator often includes.

Turning from the pattern of local house building to the question of rate subsidy, a set of reliable indicators seems relatively clear. The issue depends on the view taken of council housing. The balancing of income from rents and some contribution from the rate fund is a difficult and explosive exercise in many local authorities. As the Prices and Incomes Board observed, decisions like that made by Barrow to reduce very quickly a very high level of rate subsidy have most severe implications for council tenants. The wide range of rate subsidies, varying from those who make no contribution to those where it forms over thirty per cent of housing revenue, reflect the varying local conditions and attitudes which may be effective.

In terms of need two indicators seem relatively obvious. The extent of local council housing would be one, reflecting where it is high the commitment to this sphere of activity. Where it is low it would make the private sector more significant and the cost of council housing less severe. In any event the strength of need for a subsidy should vary with the number of council tenants. Similarly with our regular social class indicators of need. As a form of redistributive activity, the rate subsidy will penalise the better-off sections of the community and benefit the worse-off. In need terms, therefore, our two extreme class groups have the appropriate impact. This would be reinforced by the obvious importance of tenants' ability to pay when rent levels are being set. In poorer areas they will be less able and the need for subsidy will be greater.

In terms of disposition, comment has already been offered on Labour's generally favourable attitude towards council tenants. This held good for actual building and it will be interesting to see whether they also see housing costs as a legitimate charge on the general ratepayer. So far as the public and officers are concerned, disposition is a more complex phenomenon. The high public involvement in housing has been noted, but it is essentially an individual tenant relationship. There is evidence of council tenants mobilising on the issue of rents, (15) but it is not common. To the extent that the middle class are more involved one might even expect participation to create lower subsidies. Officer impact is complicated by the necessary interaction of those who built the houses, those who manage them and the treasurer's staff. All three might have very different views on the issue of subsidies. More importantly, the political significance of the decision no doubt militates against officer impact and in favour of councillors. At any rate our usual indicators will be used to test for a relationship.

The resource question, exclusively financial, is also rather complicated. High local tax resources would seem to be necessary to generous rate subsidies. This will obviously be affected by other pressures for spending, especially when an alternative means of finance is available in the form of rents. The implication of this alternative source of financing is increased by the availability of rent rebate schemes where higher rents create hardship, though similar provisions now also apply to local rates. Generally, however, one expects higher resource levels to be associated with higher

67

subsidies, though remembering our earlier cases, other factors may invert this relationship.

The simple relationships between these indicators and the level of rate subsidy are shown in Table 6-4. Need is shown to be related, though the relationship between the volume of council housing and the rate subsidy merits somewhat closer attention. Disposition is also very closely related, at least in party political terms. The low relationship with other disposition indicators should not be interpreted as implying the absence of public and official effect, as the indicators are not ideal. They do, however, operate in the hypothesised directions, even though only weakly. Finally, resource measures show strong relationships in every case. As before, however, there are many problems with these simple relationships in addition to interpreting the inverse relationship with council tenancies. Interrelationships are obvious among the independent variables and need to be sorted out by the partialling technique.

Table 6-4. Simple correlations between level of Rate Subsidy to the Housing Account and selected indicators of need, disposition and resources

Indicator	Correlation
NEED	
Per cent in social classes IV & V	0.414
Per cent in social classes I & II	−0.314
Per cent of households in council houses	−0.240
DISPOSITION	
Councillor	
Per cent Labour membership on council	0.470
Public	
Per cent turn-out in local elections 1964	−0.029
Per cent turn-out in local elections 1965	−0.109
Officials	
Number of committees	0.023
Number of sub-committees	0.090
RESOURCES	
Rate deficiency grant	0.635
Rate levied	0.448
Per capita rateable value	−0.522

This is done in Tables 6-5 and 6-6. Need measured in social class terms becomes the least important of our indicators though it shows independent association in certain contexts. This aspect of need will operate independently of dispositions or resources treated individually, but their combined effect produces a reversal of the relation with class. Personal need may thus be important, though in slightly more limited circumstances than in our earlier cases. More important on the need side is the sustained negative relationship between the scale of council housing and the level of subsidy. This implies that a large stock of council houses creates less need

Table 6-5. Partial correlations between level of Rate Subsidy to the Housing Account and selected indicators of need, disposition and resources

	Controlling for			
Effect of	Class IV & V	Council housing	Labour	Grant
Class IV & V	0.414	0.558	0.131	0.105
Council housing	−0.466	−0.240	−0.505	−0.319
Labour	0.276	0.620	0.470	0.283
Grant	0.536	0.657	0.543	0.635

Table 6-6. Partial correlations between level of Rate Subsidy to the Housing Account and selected indicators of need, disposition and resources

Effect of	Controlling for					
	Class IV & V & Labour	Class & Council housing	Class IV & V & Grant	Council housing & Labour	Council housing & Grant	Labour & Grant
Class IV & V				0.252	0.287	−0.096
Council housing	−0.539		−0.407			−0.495
Labour		0.404	0.280		0.476	
Grant	0.538	0.491		0.534		

for rate subsidies which may arise for a variety of reasons. It may be that the extent of council housing reflects a long history of such building and consequently a substantial body of older and cheaper houses. The reduced burden of such housing in terms of the housing account might make the subsidy less necessary. On the other hand, it could be that the extent of housing would create such a burden in subsidy terms that the authority does not undertake to subsidise at all. The cost implications of a large percentage subsidy in a large account could be quite dramatic. Yet again it may simply mean that the rationale of spreading housing costs to the community as a whole by rate subsidy falls down when the dominant property groups are council tenants. Whatever the explanation the negative relationship is very clear. Other things being equal, the scale of local authority housing is inversely related to rate subsidies.

Disposition is also independently related if one retains only the party measure for this. Labour councils continue to pay higher subsidies whatever the extent of need or the availability of resources. Here is further evidence of a generalised welfare commitment operating in a relatively undifferentiated way. This would square with the criticism often levelled at Labour councils that they tend to use provisions such as subsidies in a rather broad, unselective manner.

Finally, these tables also show resources as being relevant, though again in the rather indirect way which has characterised our previous cases. Poorer authorities, as measured by the level of rate deficiency grant, are much more likely to pay high rate subsidies. Again one does not argue from this that lack of resources causes expenditure but that there is a close connection between the two. What is important about the relationship is its implication in cost terms for other services. It reflects the general pattern for housing already noted, where poor local authorities are the biggest spenders. It also confirms, because of the measure which has been used, that differential central aid is probably crucial in allowing such authorities to enjoy high levels of expenditure. In terms of our earlier concerns in Chapter 1, it throws some doubt on the idea that central funds necessarily involve central control.

Thus we have two aspects of housing of a general nature showing similar broad relationships. Needs, dispositions and resources are all relevant to the level of activity adopted. These relationships are very similar to those which we found for education in the previous chapter. The implication of these relationships for much cheaper residual services now remains to be considered. Such residual services, because cheaper, are perhaps more marginal to disposition and amenable to more varied pressure.

70

7 Personal Social Services

Housing and education are invariably regarded as social services, but have been given separate treatment here because of their inordinate importance in both financial and substantive terms. Comments will be offered later on the appropriateness of classifying them with the other social services, but in the meantime attention will be diverted to the more traditional of such services. These are in some sense basic to the whole idea of the welfare state, particularly in its local government context. They are underpinned by three of the major postwar Acts of Parliament which framed the contemporary welfare state. They are the welfare and children's services and some aspects of the local health services. In terms of the latter, such things as sewage disposal and cleansing are not included, attention being focused on the more personal health services. The common elements between these services are then considerable in terms of general orientation, type of staff employed, nature of work and so on. The case for treating them together, and seeing them as similar, has been increased by the proposals in the Green Paper about the National Health Service(1) and by the Seebohm Report on the personal social services. The recommendation of the latter for a new department, with

> 'responsibilities going beyond those of existing local authority departments, but [to] include the present services provided by children's departments, the welfare services provided under the National Assistance Act 1948, educational welfare and child guidance services, the home help service, mental health social work services, other social work services provided by the health department, day nurseries, and certain social welfare work currently undertaken by some housing departments'(2)

clearly confirms the unified and uniform nature of the services that are being considered here. Such an unequivocal call for a structural change in local government gives added interest to any findings about these services and the factors which affect their operation. The argument for a departmental merger has to be seen against the fact that some of these services were at one time carried on within a single department and that some still are.(3) The fact that in some cases they have been separated out over the past ten years raises many questions about why such a separation should occur, but also about the viability of any new collective arrangements. The criteria for amalgamation of these services implicit in Seebohm are very much based on the 'pure' social work approach. It is argued that these services share a common approach and method of operation which gives them an essential unity. The fact that they have not always been seen in this way may account for the recent removal of welfare functions from the local Health Departments, and have been partly responsible for the statutory separation of Children's Departments.(4) It may have been necessary in 1948 to create distinct Children's Departments to direct adequate attention to that aspect of the social services. Similarly, when Welfare was subsumed under Health it may not have been obvious that it was receiving parity of esteem or treatment with other aspects of local health activity. In the first case, it is difficult to test the impact of the change, as before 1948 provision was much less and information is lacking. On the question of Welfare, the Seebohm Committee was not convinced of the improvements brought by separation from Health.(5) The problems of allocation within a department simply become problems between departments and success may depend on a large array of authority characteristics. Separate existence may strengthen the claims of Welfare staff but it will not remove the implied professional differences between them and Medical Officers. It is hoped that the analysis offered here may clarify some of the issues involved in this argument.

While the three services are obviously similar in many respects, they do tend to cater for discrete clienteles and their commonalities and differences need to be echoed in any explanatory scheme which is offered. The variation in the clients served is at the heart of our concept of need, at least on the personal side. Though these are essentially individual services it will be assumed that the aggregate characteristics of a community will directly reflect the likely incidence of such individual needs. Each of the services caters for personal inadequacies of one sort or another, but they vary in the type of inadequacy and its root causes.

Thus ill-health of one sort or another will engage the Health Department far more than either of the other two. At the same time, the work of the maternity services and, in part, of the Health Visitors will involve that department with a similar clientele to that encountered by Children's. Indeed the direct relation of the latter to the child population may be mitigated somewhat by the family orientation which is becoming more prevalent in the children's service. Welfare perhaps stands somewhat apart, catering mainly for the aged and the handicapped, particularly the former. In very general terms the Health Service is universal in its scope, though some kinds of treatment may be sectional and more important. The other two are much more obviously sectional in their scope but cater for the opposite ends of the population in age terms.

While age structure is important for two of the services, it can be argued that social composition has an impact on all three. Need for all the various personal health services will be higher among the less well-off sections of the community.(6) This characteristic would also seem likely to reinforce need for the other two services as well. It will be the less well-off and old people who need the relevant services most. As the census basis of social classification combines a measure of occupation and income it may be taken to reflect both personal and financial competence reasonably accurately. Each of these is likely to create a need for local authority social services.

Such personal factors do not of course operate in isolation from the physical environment. Crowded housing conditions, absence of household

72

amenities and related physical problems tend to create personal problems of their own as well as emphasising the difficulties of people within the personal categories which have been mentioned. People who would be able to cope by themselves in reasonable housing fail to do so because of this additional problem. It is the recognition of this fact which encourages social workers to support housing efforts and many other forms of amenity provision which have no direct social implications. This may have serious results, if we are right in seeing local authorities as allocators of resources between services. The social worker who supports expenditure on housing may be encouraging an allocation which leaves less to be spent on his own direct activity. The officer concerned with housing does not face this sort of ambiguity, which may strengthen his claims in the competition for funds. This problem may be accentuated by the fact that the social worker exercises little apparent influence over the way in which housing funds are spent. The Seebohm Committee recognised this very clearly in their call for more preventive work and for the involvement of social work staff in decisions about these related areas.(7)

But while need is relatively obvious in connection with these social services, the other parts of our scheme are somewhat less so. Disposition in political terms has become increasingly obscured over the years by the much wider acceptance by all parties of the case for government provision of social services. Our measures of expenditure, however, though for only one recent year, are intended to reflect a general pattern among authorities and it therefore seems reasonable to suppose that the traditional party distinction will be relevant. The Labour Party is thus hypothesised as being more favourably disposed towards these services, in part because of the way they have developed and the party's role in that development,(8) also because of the Labour view which favours a larger role for government, and the fact that the party often relates more directly to those sections of the population for whom these services cater. As these are essentially redistributive services, though less obviously than the more expensive ones already considered, they will tend to divide the parties along traditional lines. The recent blurring of this distinction which has been remarked may be modifying the conflict, though it seems likely that a division will remain about standards of need and desirable levels of provision. This pattern seems common to all the social service fields as the fact of government provision becomes more legitimate and accepted by all parties.

Again, as with the first two services discussed, measures of officer disposition and popular attitudes are difficult to obtain. In terms of the second, the wide array of voluntary organisations which cater for many personal social problems is an important element though not easy to interpret. While such groups may be seen as evidence of considerable popular mobilisation,(9) they can impinge on the local authority in two quite different ways. They may operate as substitute providers of services in the social service field, and the little evidence which is available suggests that this is their most common role. As the evidence to the Maud Committee showed, councillors are well disposed towards voluntary activity and are substantially in favour of a combination of council and voluntary work to meet new and developing needs. This argues strongly in favour of voluntary bodies as allies of, and substitutes for, local authorities, which may broadly subdue their pressure for wider council provision. Such a view is reinforced by the fact that there are few objections to voluntary work in principle, the main misgivings about it arising on grounds of efficiency and effectiveness. More effective voluntary organisations could be an even greater ally. If they do operate in this way, then it is likely that they may be found in association with a lower level of council activity, partly because they create an appearance of official action, but also because they mute the overall expression of need, both objectively and probably psychologically. On the other hand, they may operate as groups trying to stimulate government action rather than substituting for it. In this case they would probably be associated with higher levels of government activity as they are very well-developed in most areas and enjoy the support of many people active in other ways in local politics. It seems most probable, however, that this latter form of action is less common. The result is that popular attitudes may be important, but only as a general setting within which policy has to be made.

With officers the case is more complex. In Housing and Education we were dealing with separate departments, while local authority organisation in the traditional social services areas considered here is more complicated. Allocation of responsibility varies widely, both in administrative and in committee terms, as do the nomenclature and the qualifications of Chief Officers.(10) Such organisational factors may be of great significance in determining the impact of officer dispositions. Reference has already been made to the implicit view that welfare services are not guided in the same way from within Health Departments as when they are independent, though evidence is by no means clear. While this departmental structure is of importance, it remains true that there are distinguishable differences in the professional competence and impact of officers between the three services. The Welfare and Children's Departments are both relatively recent developments and the professional values of social workers are only now developing and assuming clear form. This recent development is very apparent in the lack of a clear and direct statement of the philosophy of social work within the Seebohm Report. This in itself might raise doubts among the officials concerned, but would be exaggerated by the fact that, in any case, many of the staff within these departments are not professionally qualified and might not share the developing attitudes of those who are trained. Within the Health Department there is obvious and developed professional expertise, but Seebohm raises the interesting point that the 'personal service' components may tend to be under-privileged in such departments, indicating a particular professional orientation, though again the evidence is not strong.(11) For all these reasons it seems likely that the official disposition will be less important than in a service like education, though tending to have its greatest impact on the health service.

The point has already been made that party differences may be smaller here than in housing and education. To some extent this may be due to the smaller volume of resources devoted to these three services, a factor which renders them more marginal in terms of the overall scope of govern-

74

ment, measured in financial terms. At the same time as this may bear on party disposition it is also likely to affect the relationship of local re sources to these services. They are cheaper than many other services but nevertheless involve an element of resource allocation. Because of this relative cheapness they are likely to be less related to the availability of local resources than was the case with education or housing. The health service being the biggest spender of the three should have the closest relation with financial resources. But, if the implications of finance are straightforward and limited, the availability of trained manpower seems bound to exercise some influence. The shortage of trained personnel has already been referred to and there is some evidence about the impact of skilled personnel on the work of departments.(12) It has not been possible to incorporate a measure of this resource in our analysis but its implications are relevant and must be borne in mind. In fact there is no reason to suppose a dramatic variation between authorities in terms of the availability of trained personnel and it may be that the difference between the Children's and Welfare Departments would be more significant than between them and Health.(13) Certainly it should have a bearing on the relative development of the two services.

Using a similar array of variables to that used in the previous cases, Table 7-1 shows their relationships with each of the service expenditures under consideration. In very broad terms these figures give direct support to the relationships which have just been outlined, with the strength of the relationships lower than in housing and education. Some features do merit observation, however, the most outstanding being the different kinds of relationship for the welfare service as compared with the other two. This raises interesting questions about the broad service similarities which have been observed, and these will be taken up later.

For the health and children's services the relationships closely support our scheme. Need as measured by social class is related to spending, and both services show a similar relationship with the two youngest segments of the population. In the latter case the level of relationship is not as high as one might have expected, although it is maintained for each of the two age categories. At the same time need in the physical sense shows even stronger relationships. Housing standards and the overall density of population both relate quite closely to the level of spending.

In addition to these indicators, overall population size was also included though the measures of expenditure control for this factor. It has been retained in this case because of the strong relationship which it shows to expenditure on the children's services. In our earlier services the relationship was very small. This may be explained by the relation between size and housing conditions or population density, the latter showing a high correlation. On the other hand, it may be that size creates special problems in itself. More probably, the relationship may be due to the features of larger Children's Departments which create disproportionate spending, such as more specialist services and more trained staff.(14) This would square with the fact that it is much less significant in the other two services. The overall evidence of Table 7-1 is that needs of both a physical and a personal kind are relevant to the health and children's services.

Table 7-1. Simple correlations between per capita spending on Health, Children and Welfare Services, and selected indicators of need, disposition and resources

Indicator	Correlations		
	Health	Welfare	Children
NEED			
Population size	0.111	—0.078	0.338
Per cent of population in social classes I & II	—0.282	0.022	—0.375
Per cent of population in social classes IV & V	0.255	0.006	0.237
Per cent of population aged 0-4	0.146	—0.170	0.188
Per cent of population aged 5-14	0.010	—0.189	0.205
Per cent of population aged 65 plus	—0.133	0.204	—0.227
Per cent of houses possessing standard amenities	—0.381	—0.200	—0.227
Density of population	0.215	—0.042	0.453
DISPOSITION			
Councillors			
Per cent Labour membership on council	0.330	0.007	0.314
Public			
Per cent turn-out in local elections 1964	—0.026	0.182	—0.236
Per cent turn-out in local elections 1965	—0.056	0.168	—0.233
Officials			
Number of committees	0.155	0.089	0.122
Number of sub-committees	0.158	—0.083	0.216
Employment of an O and M officer	0.022	0.072	0.018
RESOURCES			
Rate levied	0.389	0.213	0.194
Per cent of rateable value high domestic properties	—0.225	0.110	—0.221
Rate deficiency grant	0.245	0.109	0.073
Per cent rateable value domestic properties	—0.310	—0.107	—0.383

Disposition too has important effects. Councillor disposition is related to both services, confirming Labour's general orientation towards the social services. In this case, however, the other elements of disposition also show more interesting relationships, perhaps because party is somewhat less salient, or more probably because these more personalised

76

services are more responsive to non-party influences. In any event spending on the children's service is negatively correlated with electoral turnout. The greater the level of electoral mobilisation the lower the tendency to spend on this service. The relationship between party and population size and turn-out may account for this and will be dealt with later when the effects are partialled out. Most probably, however, it is an indirect effect of social composition and this too will be examined later. More interesting still are the two measures for committees with their implications about lack of officer autonomy. For both health and children's services it appears that the more elaborate councillor involvement favours higher spending. This would in fact reinforce the party relationship by creating opportunities for party to operate at lower levels of decision. On the other hand, it may be argued that extensive use of committees favours officer influence by exposing councillors to them in situations which are likely to enhance the officer's impact. The smaller relationship in the case of Welfare is interesting since much of the pressure for separate identity was designed to secure this officer position. These relationships should, however, be clarified by the subsequent partialling analysis.

Before looking at the Welfare case, the relationships with resources deserve consideration. Taking the rate and rate deficiency grant measures as most indicative, the pattern of relationships is as hypothesised. Again it is the poorest authorities who show the most marked propensity to spend on the more expensive service. In terms of the grant measure there is only a very slight relationship in the case of children's service spending. Once again it may be wiser to reserve comment until after the further analysis. It is sufficient that in the Health case there is an initial relationship worth closer examination. The other two measures which reflect the composition of the tax base reveal the expected negative relationships. Where the element which suffers from high rates is large, there is less likelihood of substantial spending on these redistributive services, as there was with the others. Such sections of the population would no doubt give generously to substitute private services, but government action tends to merit a different response.

For the welfare service, the relationships are even more interesting, because they do not conform to those for the other two services. In terms of need the age variable is most obviously connected and this is supported by the measure of household amenities. An elderly population creates an obvious need and this is enhanced by bad housing conditions, which often affect the elderly and long-term residents in an area. The absence of any reinforcement in terms of social composition may be explained by the seaside resorts which are relatively high class and cater for large numbers of old people, matched by poorer authorities with similar pressures.

Welfare is the first of our services not to show a marked relationship with Labour control and this is a most significant variation. If party is not relevant in this area, public opinion may be and electoral turn-out does show a positive correlation. None of the committee measures do, however, perhaps confirming the low professionalism and officer impact in this service. Finally, in resource terms the service falls somewhat between the other two, as does its level of spending.

Before looking at the more detailed partial correlations further comment is necessary on the variation between welfare and the other two services. Its different pattern of relationships with our independent variables is made more interesting by the interrelation of the three services. This is shown in the correlation matrix below which relates spending on each service.

	Children	Welfare	Health
Children	1. 000	0. 296	0. 456
Welfare		1. 000	0. 494
Health			1. 000

All three are positively related but most particularly health and each of the other services. In the case of the health and children's services, there is no problem as they also share other similar patterns of relationship. In the case of welfare, it is more difficult because the same relationships are not shared, or not as fully by any means.

One possible explanation for the close relation between Health and Welfare spending may lie in the organisational closeness of the two departments in many authorities. It may be that when Welfare was a sub-department of Health, its share of resource allocations was proportionate to that of the Health Department. Given some of the findings about budgetary processes one might expect this level to have been continued even after the departments were split.(15) The Seebohm Committee commissioned research into this question and found no evidence about the effectiveness of joint or separate departments.(16) While this may be true of effectiveness measured by some social service criteria, it may not be for budgetary allocations. Seebohm's hope for greater budgetary allocations to a larger social service department suggests that he was not convinced that separate departments do better than joint ones in this respect. Unfortunately the evidence in the Seebohm Report does not provide sufficient detail to test the claim being made here, as in 1966 when the data was collected the bulk of the county boroughs operated on a separate basis. In line with this interpretation of the figures, it may not be resource allocations which were at the root of pressure to divide Health and Welfare, but combinations of a genuine wish to pursue different policies which were frustrated by Medical Officers, and the wish to head independent departments on the part of Welfare Officers. Seebohm offers some support for both of these views, but one awaits a closer analysis of the politics of local budgetary allocations before making any final judgement.

Leaving this important but difficult problem for analysis elsewhere, Tables 7-2 to 7-7 explore the interrelationships among our variables by the application of partial correlation techniques to them. Taking the Welfare case first, because relationships there are more obvious from the outset, the table immediately clarifies the main factor among our chosen cluster. The need component of the population age structure maintains its

Table 7-2. Partial correlations between per capita spending on Welfare Services and selected indicators of need, disposition and resources

Effect of	Controlling for				
	Amenities	Aged 65+	Labour	Turn-out 1964	Grant
Amenities	—0.200	—0.244	—0.230	—0.205	—0.170
Aged 65+	0.247	0.204	0.256	0.204	0.242
Labour	—0.116	0.158	0.007	0.038	—0.041
Turn-out 1964	0.188	0.119	0.185	0.182	0.170
Grant	0.021	0.172	0.166	0.087	0.109

Table 7-3. Partial correlations between per capita spending on Welfare Services and selected indicators of need, disposition and resources

Effect of	Controlling for					
	Amenities & Aged 65+	Amenities & Turn-out 1964	Amenities & Grant	Aged 65+ & Turn-out	Aged 65+ & Grant	Turn-out 1964 & Grant
Amenities				—0.239	—0.191	—0.186
Aged 65+		0.195	0.257			0.249
Turn-out 1964	0.108		0.187		0.079	
Grant	0.077	—0.008		0.169		

relationship, when other need elements are controlled, and when dispositions and resources are controlled. The service would appear to be most closely related to one segment of the population, and the presence of an elderly population readily generates a higher level of expenditure. There is some evidence that the less specific indicators of need are also independently related, though the order of relationship is lower. Need in its various manifestations is clearly important.

The same cannot be said for disposition and resources. The relationship between welfare spending and party varies considerably when the other factors are controlled, and is never very high. This is not surprising in view of the very low level of simple relationship found in Table 7-1. One interesting feature, however, is that party does have a bearing once need is controlled. Given no special pressures of need, Labour councils are more favourable to this aspect of the social services, as they were to education and housing. The other correlations suggest that this may be accounted for by some other local features.

Popular disposition as measured by voting turn-out does, however, appear to be significant. Though only moderately related in Table 7-1, it retains an independent relationship when needs are controlled, despite some of our indicators of need being related to voting turn-out. It also retains this independent relation when other dispositional factors are controlled and when resources are held constant. This suggests a popular impact on the service, perhaps because of its low party salience, or perhaps because this service is highly organised in the voluntary sphere. This would argue against our analysis of voluntary impact, unless their major technique is to solicit funds from the local authority which would increase spending. While need has a direct bearing it can obviously be strengthened where popular interest is available to be mobilised in its cause.

In the case of resources, the level of rate deficiency grant shows only limited independent relationship when needs and dispositions are controlled. Given a state of need and a degree of public involvement, however, there is a tendency for poorer authorities to spend more.

Thus one finds a service responding to its clientele, but not relating as strongly to our other factors. Resources are not vitally at stake because of the low cost of the service, but may become important in certain circumstances. Parties are not closely involved because the service is not a major aspect of government work, and perhaps because the influence within parties of the particular client groups is very small. The old and the handicapped seem unlikely to mobilise many resources to affect the dispositions of politicians, though there is much symbolic party support for the aged. It is this support which is probably caught by our indicator of public disposition and which would account for its only moderate impact. Perhaps this is simply the inevitable lot of services which are marginal to local activity in the broad sense, and which in addition only affect marginal segments of the population. If this is the case then one might predict changes in the future as the rising age structure of the population of many authorities make its impact felt. Our data suggest that this will bring a direct increase in expenditure, which may in time bring increasing party interest in this area of service. On the other hand, the combination of all the social services into one department may give them the collective impact which they lack individually, a view which very clearly underlies much of the Seebohm Report.

Turning to Tables 7-4 and 7-5 it is clear that the relationships affecting the children's service are somewhat different from the welfare case, and suggest that welfare services as currently understood may not do as well in joint departments. A number of the measures show much clearer relationships here, supporting the view that pressures may be more obvious and therefore more likely to be met in this service.

Table 7-4. Partial correlations between per capita spending on Children's Services and selected indicators of need, disposition and resources

Effect of	Controlling for								
	Class IV & V	Amenities	Population size	Labour	Grant	Aged 0-4	Aged 5-14	Turn-out 1964	Number of sub-committees
Class IV & V	0.237	0.080	0.255	0.022	0.235	0.167	0.140	0.191	0.209
Amenities	-0.273	-0.348	-0.339	-0.225	-0.354	-0.332	-0.320	-0.356	-0.398
Population size	0.350	0.329	0.338	0.331	0.357	0.323	0.343	0.271	0.307
Labour	0.213	0.162	0.306	0.314	0.314	0.263	0.246	0.290	0.248
Grant	-0.069	-0.101	0.141	-0.072	0.073	0.009	-0.005	0.109	0.062
Aged 0-4	0.084	0.152	0.157	0.061	0.174	0.188	0.057	0.140	0.168
Aged 5-14	0.071	0.147	0.214	0.041	0.192	0.101	0.205	0.171	0.199
Turn-out 1964	-0.190	-0.248	-0.210	-0.202	-0.249	-0.201	-0.208	-0.236	-0.206
Number of sub-committees	0.185	0.295	0.159	0.166	0.213	0.199	0.211	0.182	0.216

Table 7-5. Partial correlations between per capita spending on Children's Services and selected indicators of need, disposition and resources

Effect of	Controlling for									
	Amenities & Population size	Amenities & Labour	Amenities & Turn-out 1964	Amenities & Sub-committees	Population size & Labour	Population size & Turn-out	Population size & Sub-committees	Labour & Turn-out 1964	Labour & Sub-committees	Turn-out 1964 & Sub-committees
Amenities					−0.219	−0.344	−0.330	−0.248	−0.226	−0.344
Population size	0.158	0.327	0.256	0.289		0.296	0.285	0.277	0.309	0.251
Labour			0.126	0.120		0.296	0.285			0.267
Turn-out 1964	−0.128	−0.227		−0.208	−0.075		−0.110		−0.181	
Number of sub-committees	0.137	0.168	0.155		0.110	0.149		0.140		

The first point to note from the tables is that need is an important factor, though the main agents of need are initially surprising. The age structure of the population shows a varied relationship but is important. Significantly, however, it shows little relationship when party is controlled, confirming the importance of disposition in relation to this aspect of need. The same is true of the social class factor, though it also is reduced when physical conditions are controlled. In spite of the personal nature of the service these two findings both suggest that physical factors may be important. Rather obvious broad patterns of personal need are less salient than more measurable local conditions which are perhaps more prone to professional interpretation; or more useful as levers with which to move councillors to take decisions.

This is confirmed by the clear independent relationship between spending and the quality of local housing and the size of the population. The first confirms the degree to which the quality of the physical surroundings can affect personal services. It also confirms the likely value of much of the preventive work recommended in the Seebohm Report. The other factor is the size of the local population, and again it must be stressed that the dependent variable is a per capita measure and thus controls for size. Many explanations for the higher spending of large authorities are offered in the literature, from the capacity to carry many specialist services to the cost problems of very large case loads. It is not possible with our data to judge on this issue, though evidence from other sources tends to suggest some conflicting pressures.(17)

If, as was suggested earlier, however, one takes higher spending as indicative of greater service, then this relationship has serious consequences. Much of the current attitude about personal services such as this one indicates a consensus in favour of small units of operation. According to our evidence this would tend to produce a less generous allocation of resources to the service, though of course it might produce better client relationships because of the closeness of small-scale working. Current recommendations appear to accept the argument for size, but the case is by no means conclusive.

In terms of the disposition element, two features are of obvious importance. One is the greater relevance of party in this case than in the welfare one, though the relationship is not as strong as in our earlier services. This pro-Labour relationship may be due to the same set of attitudes which showed Labour councils favouring expenditure on education: that is, it may be due to a much more general commitment related to the increasing family focus of the service, which might also explain the lower salience of the age structure. It might be that Labour councils are more oriented towards the needs of young couples than are Conservative ones, with council housing being a parallel case.

The other feature also concerns this relation with Labour control, but a different point needs to be stressed. The relationship here, compared with the almost complete absence of a relation for welfare, suggests a dispositional difference between two services of basically similar kind. This means that any development of a joint social services department will have to account for a political control which may be favourable to one section of the new department more than another. This might lead to differential allocation of resources within any new department, to the detriment of many advantages hoped for by the advocates of change. It might be that welfare sections will suffer as much in social service departments as they once did in some Health Departments.

A further dispositional element also shows an independent relationship, namely the voting turn-out, but the relationship is a negative one. An active population, at least in this sense, is thus seen to relate to lower expenditure on this service. Whether this means that those who are active favour other services or that those who are active tend to provide in this kind of field, thus reducing the need for council action, is not clear. Either would explain the finding, but so might a number of other factors, though the relationship remains independently of high social composition.

The measure of resources, as one would expect, shows only a weak independent relationship. This is consistent with the low cost of the service which absorbs only a small proportion of local spending. To the extent that a relationship does show, it is perhaps worth noting that it is inverted when other factors are controlled. Other things being equal, wealthier authorities spend more on this service than the poorer authorities, a reversal of the relationship in our earlier cases. While not very important in itself, it does tend to confirm the idea expressed earlier that poor authorities have little slack left when deciding about the less expensive areas of service. They have used up their capability in costly areas, and at the margins are very limited.

Finally, looking at the health service, needs are related independently to spending, though, as in the case of children, it is not the personal variables which show the closest relationship. The housing amenity measure again shows a relationship independent of class, party and grant. The possible explanation of this physical relationship with each of these essentially personal services is worth considering. It may be that the personal client groups in this and the children's case are relatively small, and particularly inarticulate. This means that service activity may have to be guided by

Table 7-6. Partial correlations between per capita spending on Health Services, and selected indicators of need, disposition and resources

| Effect of | Controlling for | | | |
	Class IV & V	Amenities	Labour	Grant
Class IV & V	0.255	0.083	0.032	0.149
Amenities	−0.303	−0.381	−0.257	−0.312
Labour	0.219	0.162	0.330	0.257
Grant	0.130	0.008	0.121	0.245

need observed from within the council system, unlike education, where the statute generates the need. If this is the case then physical indicators may be a more ready indirect indication of need than the more difficult process of seeking after particular needy clients. The authorities with depressed housing may have more obvious problems, though not necessarily more problems. In addition, bad housing conditions may convert personal inadequacies into department cases, which would be saved by improved housing. If, as is sometimes argued, councillors are more persuaded by tangible arguments, then this would be a possible explanation.

Labour control is related to health spending in a consistent way when needs and resources are controlled, though the level of relationship is not high. This seems likely to be a result of the greater expense involved in the health service with its implications for the scope of government generally. There may also be an element of long-standing commitment to the community health service, related as it was to better housing in many areas and to a range of other municipal enterprises.

The other dispositional measures did not show any very marked relationships and were not analysed further. This variation from welfare and children, at least in terms of public disposition, is quite interesting. Perhaps the health services have been in existence long enough to have established an independent status. Alternatively, it may be that the medical profession enjoys less interference because of its status within the local government system and the community at large. One often has the impression that social workers are seeking similar status in order to improve their own position in local authorities. Our data suggest that this would be rational for Children's Officers, who appear disadvantaged by public involvement, but not so for Welfare Officers, for whom the public act in a supportive role. Perhaps this itself is a result of the lower professional expertise of Welfare Officers in general.

Table 7-7. Partial correlations between per capita spending on Health Services and selected indicators of need, disposition and resources

Effect of	Class IV & V & Amenities	Class IV & V & Labour	Class IV & V & Grant	Amenities & Labour	Amenities & Grant	Labour & Grant
	Controlling for					
Class IV & V				−0.017	0.051	−0.014
Amenities		−0.255	0.282			0.233
Labour	0.141		0.212		0.146	
Grant	0.059	0.117		0.050		

Resources tend to show some independent relationship to health expenditure, as one would expect with a more expensive service. Interestingly, as with our other more expensive services, it is the poorer authorities which spend most. This confirms the pressure of the more established and accepted services on local resources, and again has implications for the residual activity of local authorities.

Thus we have these social services, one more long-standing and two more recent, related in some ways, but differing considerably in others. All are susceptible to need, though the basis of need in the welfare case is very distinct and much more particular. Disposition is not highly significant but does have an influence, and one that operates, in party terms, least obviously when the service is more marginal to the overall scope of government. Public disposition seems to have very different effects in the different services. Resources are relatively unimportant in these rather cheap areas of service, their limited relationship varying with the cost of the service. One suspects, however, other kinds of resource are significant, in particular manpower. Need and disposition thus appear to be the important factors in this area, with the former predominating.

The major implication of these somewhat complicated findings probably relates to current proposals for reform. The differences between the three services are such as to make for certain kinds of problem. Pressures are much less powerful in each of these fields and this would suggest rather more officer discretion than in some services. This could produce internal conflicts in large joint departments where the social service cake is cut by groups of officers with widely divergent attitudes and varied professional status. If the Medical Officers are most firmly established this could dictate how allocations are made. A different problem emerges in the context of the scale of new local authorities. Population size shows a very varied relation to these services and any system of unitary authorities might produce diseconomies, for example in welfare. Many qualitative factors may influence this, however, and the evidence here is by no means conclusive, even though it coincides with the previous findings already mentioned.

8 Police and Fire

Having now considered five services of a broadly similar kind, it is time to turn to other services which are essentially different. This will provide a more general test for the scheme being proposed, but will also provide some basis for an understanding of important aspects of local authority work. In this chapter consideration is given to two services, police and fire, neither of which is normally conceived of as a social service, though there are occasions when the police service plays a type of welfare role. The oldest local service, the police occupy an increasingly important position, especially in urban communities. The increase in crime and the development of urban traffic on a massive scale are only the most obvious factors making the work of the police more difficult and more important. Other factors may now be emerging to emphasise these tendencies, in the shape of militant political participation or the incipient racial problems in those cities with large coloured populations. This importance is not reflected in the literature on local government or on the police, with a resulting inadequate knowledge of the factors which affect the operation of local police forces. (1) This fact has not prevented extreme steps being taken to reduce the number of forces in order to increase the efficiency of police work. The impact of these amalgamations, invariably forced through despite local opposition, and often resulting in or coinciding with dramatic changes in the type of policing employed in an area, is not yet understood. The criteria behind amalgamations are never fully clear, though size is obviously one central feature, and many factors which may be relevant are obviously not considered. Obvious gains such as more effective radio communications over optimal areas have to be set against the loss felt by some localities of their relationship with their own police force. Many of these factors are difficult and intangible, but it is hoped here to outline some of the more obvious relationships which may be involved.

The fire service is less obviously important, and receives even less attention in the local government literature. By its nature it is a service best appreciated when least active, and no one would wish for an active fire department. It is clear, however, that increasing industrialisation is creating a need for much more effective fire services. The cost of major fires is increasing, and like the police service, it seems likely that there will soon be more extensive appeals for some form of reorganisation of the fire services. In fact, of course, this may simply come with reorganisation of local government. Nor is the industrial problem the only one, as crowded housing in town centres is becoming an increasing problem with obvious physical and social repercussions. The emerging realisation of the problems is clear in the setting up of a national Fire Services College for advanced training, on similar lines to the Police College at Bramshill. American evidence suggests that the service may be much more important than is usually acknowledged here, and British attitudes may change as the cost of neglect continues to mount.

There are a number of reasons for treating these two services together. In the first place they share certain organisational characteristics. The strict hierarchy of uniformed ranks and the quasi-military discipline are shared by few other local services. The ambulance service can be similar and is organised within the fire department by some local authorities. In the second place they have in common the use of similar technical services. The principle of a central headquarters with relatively autonomous out-stations tends to be a feature of both services. During recent years the tendency has been for the similarity between the services to increase as manpower problems have produced a search for sophisticated technical solutions. (2) Another similarity lies perhaps in their common orientation towards property. This is obvious in the case of the fire service where there is seldom any visible client relationship, except perhaps in the context of preventive services. It is also very obvious in the way in which local areas are classified for fire risk in order to determine effective servicing levels. (3) The police provide a less obvious case, but there is perhaps a tendency for their actions to reflect the emphases of the legal system which protects property very consciously. While the detection rate for offences against the person is higher, this may reflect their smaller volume and their easier solution, but as Ben Whittaker has pointed out, 'It might be preferable if all assaults were penalised more heavily, so that the law protected persons as strongly as it protects property.'(4) Here then are two traditional services, each with an hierarchical and uniformed staff structure, using advanced equipment and operating only very indirectly with any personal clientele.

In terms of our explanatory scheme a number of factors important for both services are fairly obvious. Despite their non-client relationship, one might expect to find some relationships with need on the personal side. The long-standing animosity between the police and the working class and the fact that the traditional criminal type comes from such a background, suggests that class may be indicative of need. (5) On the other hand, the extent of crimes against property may also indicate that upper class authorities will have more to protect and therefore greater need. (6) This relationship with class depends entirely on the angle from which one sees the problem, but each orientation reinforces the other in this case. The changing nature and increased sophistication of many crimes may be changing these relationships, though this will have more effect on future relationships than on those we are dealing with. In terms of the fire service, a somewhat similar, though even less significant relationship, probably exists on the personal side. Lower class populations should not in themselves generate needs, though their association with industrialisation may create a spurious relationship. Upper class populations, given their property attachment, may create a need for fire protection, but this is more a feature of the property than of the residents. Fire departments will probably respond to property at risk as their own professional decision, though this may be aided by personal pressures on the part of residents.

On the more obvious physical side a number of factors are probably operating. In the case of the fire service, two appear most likely to be prominent. One of these concerns the incidence of different kinds of property which will have a bearing on fire risk. Assuming that industrial areas will present greater needs a measure is used for the element of rateable value taken up by domestic hereditaments. Though this involves conflating industrial, commercial and crown property into the remaining category, each of these contains elements of considerable risk and consequent need for available cover. (7) The other physical pressure is likely to arise from the density of the population, with its obvious impact on fire risk. The incidence of fires may not be higher in more crowded conditions but the results can be much more devastating. For the police service the factors influencing need are likely to be different. Given the correlation of crime with social conditions it might be expected that the lower class relationship, referred to earlier, would be reinforced by bad housing conditions. The measures of density of occupation and availability of standard amenities have been used to assess this aspect of need. The other physical need may involve the quality of domestic property, reinforcing the higher social class relationship already mentioned. The proportion of domestic hereditaments with values of over £100 has been taken as indicating the extent of property at risk, though commercial premises are also major targets.

Disposition and resources are less easy to assess in connection with these services. In the case of our major disposition indicator, party control, the probable relationships with these services are not entirely obvious. Given that these are traditional, house-keeping, order-maintaining functions, however, with little welfare content and with property orientations, it seems reasonable to assume a favourable Conservative attitude towards them. Labour councils might not actively oppose such services but would almost certainly accord them lower priority than the services which have already been considered. This would invariably mean lower expenditures. Total cash resources are not unlimited and the low priority of these services for Labour would make high spending almost impossible. Only a very wealthy, or an unusual, Labour authority could spend a lot on such low priorities and such authorities are rare. If the idea of marginality was relevant to the smaller social services it seems even more probable that services like police and fire will be still closer to the margin for Labour councils.

In terms of the other two aspects of disposition evidence is slight but commonsense interpretations suggest fairly straightforward relationships. It is unlikely that either of these services is prone to public involvement or pressure. The fire service is probably immune by virtue of its technical nature and its intermittent activity. The police service is immune because of the normative consensus that such regulatory activities should not be exposed to popular pressures. It is for just this reason that the British often pride themselves on the police not being a political matter, though our view is that this is too narrow a view of politics. Recent campaigns for 'law and order' suggest a change in this view. If public attitudes are not too significant, however, the role of the professionals may be more so. The nature of both services is such as to make them more immune from non-professional influences of all kinds and the attitudes of the officers in both services may be very important. This has traditionally been reinforced by the special status of Watch Committees, with their seniority and autonomy in relation to police matters. Both are subject to professional inspection at national level which might help such a tendency, and the Home Office pressure on appointments of Chief Constables would be a further contributory factor in the police case. (8) Attempts to strengthen this professional element are obvious in the two national colleges which have already been mentioned. Again these official dispositions can only be accounted for indirectly but they are important factors to be borne in mind during our analysis.

Resources in these service areas are more important than they were in those considered in the last chapter. Police ranks third among our services in terms of cost which in spite of the fifty per cent central grant gives it considerable financial significance. The fire service is much less expensive and one would expect a much lower relationship with resources. In addition to this obvious financial difference manpower resources would also show a different relationship. The police suffer from a shortage of staff which affects the fire service much less severely. One of the pressures for rationalisation of areas was the hope of technical developments which would alleviate the acute shortage of staff, though the process is not straightforward. Unfortunately this factor is also beyond the scope of the immediate analysis here which will be restricted to the standard financial resource indicators.

Table 8-1 shows the relationships between the police and fire service expenditures and their varied indicators of need, disposition and resources. A number of relationships appear important from this table though not always those one had hypothesised. Need is relevant but not uniformly so and relates quite differently to the two services. Personal need shows up quite distinctly, with police spending reflecting higher social composition. The protective notion would seem to be operating. In the fire service case, despite expectations to the contrary, there is a strong correlation with low social class.

A possible explanation for this appears among the physical indicators. Authorities in which the rateable value is less domestic and where valuations are lower also show a clear relationship with fire service spending. This itself correlates with low social class and the partialling technique may help to decide how much this interaction matters. Other physical indicators are also related. Contrary to our suggestion, the density of the population is related to the police service and crowding has an effect on fire service expenditure. Each of these may represent the 'ghetto' or the crowded council development, which gives them added importance.

One other feature on the need side deserves attention. Population size was again included, in spite of the dependent variable being a per capita measure. In both cases the relationship was clear, larger authorities favouring higher police and lower fire service expenditure. This reversal of the relationships is unusual given the broad similarities of the services, but repeats the relationship with social class mentioned already. Explanatory possibilities arise which involve economies and diseconomies of scale but we have no evidence about either of these. Alternatively it may be that the relation with size is a product of other features associated with a large

Table 8-1. Simple correlations between per capita spending on Police and Fire Services and selected indicators of need, disposition and resources

Indicator	Correlation	
	Fire	Police
NEED		
Population size	−0.234	0.398
Per cent of population in social classes I & II	−0.325	0.189
Per cent of population in social classes IV & V	0.497	0.011
Crowding index per room	0.158	0.023
Density of population per acre	0.059	0.266
Per cent of houses possessing standard amenities	−0.259	−0.038
Per cent of rateable value high domestic properties	−0.272	0.290
Per cent of rateable value domestic	−0.208	0.080
DISPOSITION		
Councillors		
Per cent Labour membership on council	0.239	−0.226
Public		
Per cent turn-out in local elections 1964	0.047	−0.110
Per cent turn-out in local elections 1965	−0.012	−0.027
Official		
Number of committees	−0.147	0.053
Number of sub-committees	−0.030	0.046
Employment of an O and M officer	0.162	−0.006
RESOURCES		
Level of rate	0.132	0.143
Rate deficiency grant	0.344	−0.142

population. Our subsequent analysis should tell us something about this, but these are obviously most important questions.

In the case of disposition neither the indicators of popular involvement nor of officer impact show any great relationship, though in the fire service case higher spending is associated with officer autonomy, even if only slightly. Both of these confirm our initial hypotheses though not very strongly. This weakness may be due to the inadequate measures or may reflect a genuine low impact. Of more interest is the measure of council disposition which shows reverse relationships with these two services. Fire service expenditure is directly related to the Labour percentage on the council, adding yet another service to the array in which this was the case, though again a cheap one. Police spending, on the other hand, despite its scale shows the opposite relationship. This suggests that Conservative councils may not be low-spenders, as our earlier cases seemed to suggest, but rather selective spenders with different priorities.

Before doing a partial analysis some comment on the relationships with resources is necessary. Taking the level of grant as the major indicator, police spending is a feature of wealthier authorities. This is as one would expect for an expensive service, though our previous cases have proved very different. Spending on the fire service, on the other hand, is very much a feature of poorer authorities, using this measure. This again must await the partial analysis as it is inherently unlikely that low resources actually cause high spending, particularly as they are closely related to a number of features defined as constituting need.

These partial relationships are examined in Tables 8-2 to 8-5 below. Taking the fire service case first the table clarifies a number of relationships. The most outstanding feature is the consistent independent relation of the two main indicators of need. The social class relationship is especially strong with controls for each other variable. Less strong, but equally consistent, is the inverse relationship between size and spending. The level of industrialisation, hypothesised as a very important relationship, does not maintain an independent relationship when controlled for social class, which raises some explanatory problems. The relationship with size seems almost certainly a product of the minimum cost for running a fire brigade at all. If necessary basic provision is costly then the diseconomies of small-scale working could be a prominent factor.

More difficult to explain is the apparent impact of a low class population and the absence of an independent relationship with the main physical indicators. This conflicts with our earlier assumptions. One possible explanation is that this is not an indicator of need at all, but that the working class are very favourably disposed towards the fire service. Such a view

Table 8-2. Partial correlations between per capita spending on the Fire Service and selected indicators of need, disposition and resources

| | Controlling for | | | |
| | | | | |
Effect of	Class IV & V	Size of population	Labour	Grant
Class IV & V	0.497	0.509	0.478	0.393
Size of population	−0.204	−0.234	−0.263	−0.189
Labour	−0.183	0.266	0.239	0.108
Grant	0.101	0.317	0.275	0.344

would suggest that this disposition would be more apparent in smaller towns, but when population is controlled the class impact is enhanced. It is possible that local pride in working-class authorities relates to the fire service, whereas in middle-class communities it may be the art gallery or the concert hall. Another possibility is that fire service spending is closely related to the degree of trade union organisation in the service, which would probably relate closely to class composition. Unionisation could enhance labour and related costs and cause them to escalate. However, these are only speculative suggestions as more data would be needed for a more certain judgement.

Leaving this very incomplete explanation, the partial correlations give some support to our earlier notions. Partialling out the class element converts the party relationship into an inverse one. Labour councils are related to fire service spending because of their association with working class communities. In their own right Conservative councils are more likely to favour this element of expenditure. This suggests that Labour councils devote resources in many social service directions willingly, but that here their spending is a derivation of their main electoral support. This might create many more problems were this an expensive service. Labour councils can afford to accede to such pressures while accommodating its other claims, because the resource impact is only small.

This factor is again relevant when one looks at the partial correlations with the level of resources. Poorer authorities do spend more on this service when the other factors are controlled, though the need elements have a significant bearing on this. Controlling for class does reduce the impact of the grant relationship quite significantly, and when size is also added it becomes almost negligible. Again it does not seem likely that low

Table 8-3. Partial correlations between per capita spending on the Fire Service and selected indicators of need, disposition and resources

Effect of	Controlling for					
	Class IV & V & Size of population	Class IV & V & Labour	Class IV & V & Grant	Size of population & Labour	Size of population & Grant	Labour & Grant
Class IV &V				0.472	0.422	0.420
Size of population		−0.248	−0.250			−0.212
Labour	−0.157		−0.192		0.145	
Grant	0.051	0.117		0.145		

resources cause greater spending, but that low cost services, coupled with these authorities' differentially high central grants, permit higher spending. This is in spite of the high level of spending which may already have been incurred in other costly fields.

Here then we have a service for which political disposition is not highly salient and in which resources are only marginally at issue. Needs in the form of size and social composition are able to dictate spending because of this low salience and cost marginality. We are not in a position to say more about the operation of the social class factor, but it is sufficiently unusual to suggest a fruitful area of study. The impact of trade unionism within the local government service might repay examination in terms of its impact on expenditure patterns and its relation to the class structure of the population.

The police service figures show more clear relationships, as one might expect given the importance in overall cost terms of the two services. Clearest of all is the relation of need, especially as measured by population size and density. These remain independently of other indicators of need and of dispositions and resources. On the relationship with density there is no reason to suppose that this does not reflect the enhanced social problems which this characteristic suggests. Their impact on the police service would be relatively obvious and the need for more spending clearly apparent. The question of size is more difficult. Apart from the possibilities already broached it could be that larger cities developed their police services earlier and hence traditionally spend much more. More detailed investigation would be desirable however, particularly as the current tendency is towards large police force areas. It is important to know whether our relationship simply means more spending or better policing or both. In this connection it is reassuring to note the very strong ($r =$

Table 8-4. Partial correlations between per capita spending on the Police Service and selected indicators of need, disposition and resources

Effect of	Controlling for				
	Class I & II	Size of population	Population density	Labour	Grant
Class I & II	0.189	0.242	0.312	0.021	0.142
Size of population	0.422	0.398	0.326	0.428	0.383
Population density	0.361	0.117	0.266	0.355	0.270
Labour	−0.228	−0.282	−0.328	−0.226	−0.185
Grant	−0.068	−0.081	−0.150	−0.051	−0.142

Table 8-5. Partial correlations between per capita spending on the Police Service and selected indicators of need, disposition and resources

Effect of	Controlling for									
	Class I & II & Size of population	Class I & II & Population density	Class I & II & Labour	Class I & II & Grant	Size of population & Population density	Size of population & Labour	Size of population & Grant	Population density & Labour	Population density & Grant	Labour & Grant
Class I & II					0.304	0.038	0.231	0.103	0.276	0.011
Size of population		0.319	0.428	0.419				0.329	0.307	0.428
Population density	0.222		0.367	0.355		0.214	0.126			0.352
Labour	-0.153	-0.148		-0.120	-0.331		-0.276		-0.295	
Grant	0.034	-0.008	-0.048		-0.093	0.054		-0.005		

—0. 814) inverse relationship between spending and the population per policeman. At least one important qualitative indicator of the police service is related to spending.

The other indicators of need are perhaps less important, though they show varied independent relationships. Class fails to reveal any relationship independent of party control and this seems to be a more important consideration. On the other hand, the quality of housing is related independently, at any rate when measured by our rateable value indicator. Interpretation of this latter factor is a little difficult as it could be taken to relate indirectly to disposition. Such property generates a need for the police service, but the ratepayers are obviously disposed to favour police expenditure. The need element is perhaps of greater significance as our public disposition measures are not related.

Party as a dispositional factor retains a much greater independent relationship than might have been expected. Indeed its level is quite high when resources are controlled and when size is taken as the indicator of need. This is less so in the case of the class indicator of need, as one would expect given the class-party relationship. It seems unlikely that this party relationship springs from any single aspect of the service, but its controlling regulative aspect is obviously important, in terms of traditional Conservative attitudes. Once again it is only possible to surmise because of the parties' rather broad and unspoken dispositions towards the service. This makes precise analysis of party positions difficult. It does seem likely, however, that this is a marginal service for Labour, perhaps even more so than the fire service, despite its greater costs. Labour councils may not be against police expenditure, but rather treat it as a low priority, which may be neglected in a world where cash resources are short and numerous more pressing priorities exist. Conservative councils view the service favourably as befits their law and order traditions.

Our resources' indicator itself shows virtually no relationship at all when needs and disposition are held constant. This tends to reinforce the point just made about the parties. Police expenditure is not directly related to local resources, because it depends more on how money is being spent in other areas. If the need is present or the disposition right, money will be spent, but unlike our earlier services, these are not features of poorer authorities. In the absence of these pressures, spending may depend on other priorities and their impact.

The police service is thus not like the fire service. It is susceptible to very different needs in terms of population, and it is also subject to more party influence than is the case with the fire service, though each relates to the same party. This does not tally with the traditional non-political view of the police service, though the argument may be couched in less ideological party tones than it is for other services. Ben Whittaker has applauded the fact that 'the police have never become a party political issue in this country', (9) but our evidence here suggests that Labour councils tend to be less able or willing to spend on the police service. It may not be political in the pejorative sense in which he uses the term, but the development of the service may have been affected by the prevailing pattern of urban political control.

Any effort to treat these two services together, and this is often suggested, would need to be carefully considered. Larger units may benefit both services, but only if the interpretations of our relationships with size are different for each service. If both reflect diseconomies, of large scale for the police and of small scale for fire, then medium-sized authorities might be best. On the other hand, if expenditure does reflect service perhaps they should not be run together at all. In the same way, political control and population composition could dramatically affect effort on the two services.

9 Libraries

Finally, it is necessary to turn in yet another direction to complete our
range of services and account for a further type of local government service. It has become increasingly commonplace over the last seventy years
for local authorities to provide a wide range of amenities. Parks and playing fields are one obvious provision, and libraries and museums are now
reasonably universal. Art galleries, concert halls, and civic concerts and
similar less general amenities (at least in their use if not in their intention)
are becoming more usual, but are still not common in local authorities. While
all of these are interesting in their own particular ways, comparative data
are not always easy to obtain about them and in some spheres the level of
expenditure is only small or occasional. As a result, the analysis here will
be restricted to the library service, which is universally provided in county
boroughs and has been so for a sufficient time for any general tendencies
in terms of local effects on the level of service to show.

One important problem in this area of amenity services was touched on
in an earlier chapter. In their nature many of these services, libraries no
less than parks or theatres, are generally available to the whole community.
It is not possible effectively to provide them for only one section of the
population, though of course physical position and other factors may act as
disincentives to use. A study of decisions about the location of branch
libraries might prove revealing in this respect. It is equally true that most
of these services, or at least those where some measure of use is possible,
are not used uniformly by the whole population for whom they are available.
Where this is the case it becomes difficult to establish whether the pro-
ducers aim to provide a general service or to cater for the major section
of the community using the service.

Because of the implications of this feature of provision it was felt
necessary to examine the use of libraries, if only in the broadest terms.
Accordingly the number of books issued per head of population in 1965-6
was related to a range of local characteristics to see if any particular user
patterns were detectable. Of course this is a measure of only limited value,
reference library usage, amenity services in the library, gramophone
record libraries, newspaper provision and the like being equally important.
However, as the Roberts Report pointed out, 'The essential function of the
public library, which should take precedence of all ancillary services, is to
supply to any reader, or group of readers, the books and related material
for which they ask'. (1) Thus, in spite of its limitations, the relationship
seemed worth pursuing and is shown in Table 9-1. Three features emerge
from these figures. The overwhelming impression is of middle class usage,
as one might have expected. This holds good when other characteristics
are substituted for class, though only the council housing one has been
included here. This was done because it may have a bearing on earlier com-

ments about the physical distribution of facilities. Many council estates have never been provided with amenities and branch libraries are a notable omission in most cases. This figure should not therefore be read as implying unwillingness to borrow books on the part of council tenants, but may simply reflect their isolation from libraries.

The other two features are the lack of relationship with continuation in full-time education. This is often seen as a likely source of enhanced pressure on library facilities. The lack of relationship may mean that those who stay on at school make use of reference facilities in the main, or it may be that schools and technical colleges cater directly for the fifteen-to eighteen-year-olds in full-time education. Whatever the explanation, there is not much evidence in the table for extensive children's borrowing either, though the figures do not indicate children's libraries separately. Indeed, apart from high social class groups being associated with borrowing, the only other positive association is with young adults.

These figures are not conclusive, and were not intended to be so. They do, however, provide some information about our concept of need. On the basis of this evidence it will be assumed that the class composition of any community will be indicative of the need for library provision, with the middle class providing the positive pressure. It may be argued that it would be desirable to provide libraries for the working-class sector of the population, but this itself is a dispositional factor. Our aim here is to locate objective indicators of need. At the moment the middle class provide this. A number of physical indicators, such as the owner-occupation figures already quoted, might also be used, but they would effectively only be substitutes for the class factor. There is no reason to suppose that physical characteristics present needs with regard to this service, though of course inadequate premises might be a consideration in some towns. The only case where the physical factors might appear is in the need for branch libraries, with their pressures on staff and stock and these one would pre-

Table 9-1 Simple correlation between per capita Book Issues and selected local characteristics, 1965-6

	Book issues
Per cent in social classes I & II	0.499
Per cent in social classes IV & V	—0.344
Per cent of population council tenants	—0.251
Per cent of population aged 15-18 in full-time education	0.077
Per cent of population aged 5-14	—0.051
Per cent of population aged 25-44	0.180
Per cent of population aged 65+	—0.030

sume are related to the size of any urban community. Accordingly, population size is included in our indicators of need.

With such needs in mind, the natural corollary in terms of disposition is that Conservative councils will be more favourably disposed towards library provision. This would seem obvious given the luxury interpretation which some would put on this service when contrasted with those services which have been treated earlier, and also in terms of the clientele of the library service. This relationship may be mitigated to some degree by the fact that Labour councils, already shown to be favourable to educational spending, might also see this as an area of provision which should be available to everyone, even though many would not use it. The party relationships might also be affected by the fact that few resources are devoted to the service and that it is consequently marginal in terms of the broad party division about the extent of government action.

Before leaving the question of disposition, the question of professional and public attitudes deserves some attention. Although a highly professional service it is doubtful whether this element has any very substantial

Table 9-2 Simple correlations between per capita spending on Library Services and selected indicators of need, disposition and resources

Indicator	Correlation
NEED	
Population size	0.101
Per cent of population in social classes I & II	0.133
Per cent of population in social classes IV & V	—0.070
Per cent of population aged 15-18 in full-time education	0.220
DISPOSITION	
Councillors	
Per cent Labour membership on council	—0.056
Public	
Per cent turn-out in local elections 1964	0.116
Per cent turn-out in local elections 1965	0.222
Officials	
Number of committees	—0.052
Number of sub-committees	—0.086
Employment of an O and M officer	—0.011
RESOURCES	
Rate levied	0.000
Per cent of rateable value high domestic properties	0.237
Rate deficiency grant	—0.049

impact. This is a marginal service in terms of the major preoccupations which might be expected to engage local authorities, and as such is probably relegated to a low place in the decisional hierarchy. It would also appear that librarians are not the most militant professional group in the local authority service, and that their professional image is not as strong as some others. There is little doubt that librarians convince their own committees about the service, but this does not imply conviction throughout the authority. Finally, one might expect the public to be a factor here as it is a service used mainly by those normally interested in, and involved with, the political system. The middle class might be expected to attempt to bring pressure for expansion of a service from which they undoubtedly benefit disproportionately.

Finally, resources would not appear to loom very large, as was observed when party was being considered. This is one of the smallest local services in monetary terms and staffing does not appear to be an excessive problem. Our data do not distinguish this, but it is possible that resources may become very significant when a new library is being considered. However, it is assumed that the few cases where this coincides with our figures will not affect the overall impressions of a cheap service.

Table 9-2 shows the relationship between our varied indicators and the level of library spending. Though generally lower than in our earlier cases, one or two of the relationships deserve comment. In terms of need, the size of population and the social composition show positive, though limited, effect. More important than either is the higher correlation between spending and pupils in full-time education after the age of fifteen. Despite our finding that this did not correlate with book issues, it does appear to have

Table 9-3 Partial correlations between per capita spending on Libraries and selected indicators of need, disposition and resources

Effect of	Controlling for					
	Class I & II	Full-time	Labour	Grant	Turn-out 1965	High domestic
Class I & II	0.133	−0.057	0.143	0.124	0.043	−0.103
Full-time	0.185	0.220	0.229	0.215	0.097	0.073
Labour	0.077	0.087	−0.056	−0.039	0.027	0.149
Grant	0.010	0.017	−0.028	−0.049	−0.045	0.103
Turn-out 1965	0.184	0.102	0.217	0.221	0.222	0.165
High domestic	0.222	0.116	0.272	0.253	0.185	0.237

an effect on provision. This may indicate an expectation of student need and with our earlier figures may imply a lag between enlightened provision and the impact of further education on library use. At any rate it is important among our indicators of need.

Dispositional measures show even fewer relationships of interest. Though the party measure supports our hypothesis the level of relationship is very small. Similarly, the committee measures imply a relationship with officer autonomy, but again it is very small. Only the measures of public disposition show much effect and these confirm our suggestion that public impact may be relevant here. This does appear to be a service in which public impact may be felt.

Resources, as one predicted, are not very closely related. If anything it is the wealthier authorities who spend most in this area, though the inverse correlation is small. This confirms most of our earlier findings about the financial implications of expenditure on services, but is not itself of great interest in this particular case. The one variable which shows a relationship here is the percentage of high value property, a surrogate for high social class composition.

Partialling out these relationships clarifies the impact of these related measures, though it leaves complex explanatory problems. In the context of need, high social class shows varied relationships but is of only secondary importance. Though it operates independently of party and of grant, other indicators of need and of disposition either reduce its relationship severely, or invert it. As Table 9-4 demonstrates even more clearly, social class does not relate independently of the needs of the school population, nor of

Table 9-4 Partial correlations between per capita spending on Libraries and selected indicators of need, disposition and resources

Effect of	Controlling for					
	Class I & II & Full-time	Class I & II & Turn-out 1965	Class I & II & High domestic	Full-time & Turn-out 1965	Full-time & High domestic	Turn-out 1965 & High domestic
Class I & II				−0.069	−0.153	−0.173
Full-time		0.146	0.134			−0.044
Turn-out 1965	0.109		0.215		0.133	
High domestic	0.183	0.248		0.126		

102

public disposition or the qualitative index of rateable value. In the same way, the percentage in full-time education beyond fifteen shows an independent relationship except when the same two measures are involved. Table 9-4 again shows that this is predominantly an effect of the rateable value measure.

Needs, therefore, do not seem to have much effect unless the incidence of high domestic valuations is seen as an indicator of need. This seems very unlikely and the continued independence of that variable and voting turn-out suggests that they may reflect a similar factor. Need does not operate independently but has to be mediated by public action. The independent relationship of turn-out supports this view. So does the effect of rateable value. Ratepayers in such property are likely to involve themselves in the system because of their need to guard against severe rate poundages. That involvement facilitates their positive, as well as negative, impact when other conditions are favourable. This appears to be one such case when need and party disposition are marginal and involved groups have an impact.

It may not be necessary, but these factors are reinforced by the low resource implications of the library service. Though it has not been possible to consider them here this analysis may also apply to related 'cultural amenities'. Such services fall at the margins of council decision in a number of respects. Their cheapness makes them marginal for the parties, and this removes some of the coherent policy direction which party can give. They thus come to depend on the extent to which a small but interested public can move the council to be concerned with, and active in, their provision. Council responses will vary according to a great many other factors, but it makes this area of activity less amenable to analysis with our rather crude measures. Such services as this are open to much more specific influences and our scheme deals better with more general factors.

10   Local Rates

The previous five chapters have revealed the varied relationships of needs, dispositions and resources to a variety of local services. As was pointed out earlier, however, there is in each case an associated decision involved which concerns the willingness to raise rate revenue to pay for such services. In a number of our service examples it was clear that service needs and associated dispositions overcame any reticence about taxation. Thus the less wealthy authorities were found spending heavily on our most expensive services. Such policies have obvious and severe rate implications. Equally, in the last chapter, it was clear that where needs and political dispositions were less operative, public impact was greater. As those involved were heavy rate-payers, it has some interest for our present concerns.

In the present chapter the rate levied will be analysed using the same technique as was applied to the substantive services. It seems reasonable to see the rate as resulting from needs, dispositions and resources in the same way as any chosen service. Need in relation to any tax can be derived from the incidence of the tax and the severity of the tax for those on whom it falls. While individuals vary in their capacity to pay, one assumes a general need to reduce the level of taxation. This need no doubt varies directly with the impact of the tax. One problem with the local rate in this context is that it does not relate directly to income. This gives the tax a regressive element which complicates any general assessment of its impact. The fact that it is a tax on property suggests that it will relate to needs on both the personal and physical dimensions.

On the one hand, it is likely that the better-off sections of the community will be affected more severely by the rate. They will certainly pay more and, in spite of the regressive nature of the rate, may pay disproportionately more. Coupled with the greater incidence of direct taxation on such groups anyway, it will be assumed here that they constitute one element of need for low rates. In physical terms the case is more obvious and direct. Two factors will be involved here. First, it will be assumed that need in our terms is primarily a phenomenon of domestic rate-payers. The ability of commercial and industrial undertakings to offset their rate costs is much higher than that of domestic rate-payers. An element is now allowed for this in the rate support grant.(1) Secondly, it will be assumed that the greater the proportion of high valued domestic properties, the greater will be the need for low rates. Such properties involve a severe rate burden for their occupants. Thus a combination of social composition and rate base will be used to measure need.

Disposition in relation to rates is complicated by the fact that a dual attitude is involved, one aspect concerning taxation and the other concerning spending decisions. One would expect Labour councils to be high taxers on both counts. They have been shown to be higher spenders, especially on the most expensive services which have been considered. This inevitably involves higher rates, and this would be reinforced by the fact that Labour councils probably have less interest in protecting those with a need for low rates. This is borne out in situations where 'rate-payer' parties and candidates appear to protect their interests. almost always from highly rated Labour councils. While this relationship is probably mitigated somewhat by the regressive nature of the rate, it seems likely to have general validity for our discussion.

The attitude of officials and the public here is more obvious than in some of the earlier substantive service contexts. One expects the public to be broadly anti-taxation, though not necessarily without the contradictory wish for an expansion of government action.(2) One expects this to be stronger among the middle class sections of the population where the service aspect is less relevant. The fact that these middle class sections are also likely to be more articulate, better informed and more involved, suggests that they are more likely to press their views than are working class groups for whom the rate is in any case less significant. This should be reflected in higher electoral turn-out which is a middle class phenomenon anyway.

Officials seem likely to be subject to greater cross-pressures than are the public. Working to expand their particular services according to their professional criteria, they will also be more aware than outsiders of the possible political implications of rate increases. They may thus be somewhat at odds with the politicians who are much more exposed to any repercussions which may follow from rate changes. The evidence for such repercussions is negligible but the consensus about their likelihood, among politicians, is fairly high. Without precise data for each authority it is impossible to say which factor in the relationship will be most important, though officers seem certain to be very aware of both. This kind of attitudinal data is not available but it is hoped that our party indicator will give some idea of the relative strength of the politicians' views about high rates. Parties in more marginal electoral situations are more likely to balance spending and rates in favour of the latter. Those with comfortable majorities are not. Officer autonomy will be assumed to imply higher rates on the professional grounds outlined earlier.

Lastly, though the rate is itself an indicator of resources, it is possible to conceive of an independent resource measure when considering the rate as a dependent variable. Essentially this reduces to a measure of the level of tax base, though this is of course affected by its constituents which affect need and disposition to tax. As in the case of spending, so here larger authorities have greater absolute resources. Adoption of a measure of per capita rateable value therefore gives a clearer indication of the relative taxable capacity of local authorities. High values mean a higher return for a given level of rate. The interaction between this factor and needs and dispositions about rates will determine the rate to be struck. Thus not all high value county boroughs levy low rates, nor is the reverse true. The relationships between our indicators of need, disposition and resources and the level of rate are outlined in Table 10-1.

This table shows clearly the strong relationships between this series

Table 10-1. Simple correlations between level of Rate Levied and selected indicators of need, disposition and resources

Indicator	Correlation
NEED	
Per cent of population in social classes I & II	−0.208
Per cent of rateable value domestic properties	−0.364
Per cent of rateable value high value domestic properties	−0.523
DISPOSITION	
Councillors	
Per cent Labour membership on council	0.441
Public	
Per cent turn-out in local elections 1964	0.080
Per cent turn-out in local elections 1965	−0.059
Officials	
Number of committees	0.013
Number of sub-committees	0.013
Employment of an O and M officer	−0.009
RESOURCES	
Rate deficiency grant	0.410
Per capita rateable value	−0.396

of local characteristics and the level of rate. Need is very closely related, both in terms of the general social class indicator and, more particularly, of the direct indicator of domestic rateable value. While these may to some extent increase the tax base, with an obvious reduction in the necessity for high taxes to obtain any given income, they also indicate a group interested in low rate levels in individual terms. Disposition is equally clear in the party case. Labour councils do levy higher rates, as was obviously bound to follow from our analysis of their levels of rate-fund spending on costly services. Our indicators of public and officer disposition do not show such relationships, however, suggesting that this most crucial area of decision is very much a political matter. This again is consistent with the pattern in the major services which have been considered.

Resources show closer relationships here than in many of our earlier cases. High per capita rateable values do mean lower rates, as would be expected, though the inverse relationship is not exceptionally strong. This echoes the relationship for domestic valuations and is further confirmed by the positive relationship with the level of rate deficiency grant. As we saw, the poor are big spenders and consequently big taxers.

Table 10-2. Partial correlation between level of Rate Levied and selected indicators of needs, disposition and resources

Effect of	Controlling for				
	Class I & II	Labour	High domestic	Grant	Rateable value
Class I & II	−0.308	0.063	0.231	−0.158	−0.158
Labour	0.337	0.441	0.135	0.322	0.322
High domestic	−0.490	−0.339	−0.523	−0.389	−0.377
Grant	0.322	0.272	0.168	0.410	0.173
Rateable value	−0.303	−0.249	−0.068	−0.130	−0.396

Though some of these relationships are rather obvious, they leave questions unanswered. If Labour councils are associated with lower property values, then either of these influences could be causing the higher rate levels. The fact that high value domestic property tends to be in Conservative areas raises other questions about the relation between property values and the level of rate. Is there a direct relationship or is it mediated through the agency of a non-Labour council? An attempt is made to sort out these relationships in Tables 10-2 and 10-3 which show the partial correlations among the set of variables with which we have been dealing.

It is clear from these tables that needs, dispositions and resources contribute independently to the level of rate which is levied. The clearest feature of the tables is the fact that Labour councils levy higher rates whatever their needs and resources. This is only to be expected given their tendency to spend heavily on the more expensive services which have been considered. The only factor which reduces this independent relationship is the presence of domestic property carrying high valuations, but it does not reduce it altogether.

It is difficult to interpret this factor as several of the indicators used here may be seen as either needs or resources depending on one's point of view. Following the pattern of our earlier cases, however, and taking the rate deficiency grant as a resource indicator there is an obvious relationship. Poor authorities do levy higher rates in order to compensate for their lack of rateable value, though whether differential grants assist them is difficult to say from these data. This view is confirmed by the figures for per capita rateable value which show a strong negative relationship.

This is reduced, however, when set against the other resource indicators and the fact of high valued property becomes most significant. It is obvious that some of its impact on the rate level is a result of its resource component. Authorities with such a pattern of rateable values are almost certainly better-off and can raise equivalent sums by levying lower rates,

Table 10-3. Partial correlations between level of Rate Levied and selected indicators of need, disposition and resources

Controlling for

Effect of	Class I & II & High domestic	Class I & II & Labour	Class I & II & Grant	Class I & II & Rateable value	High domestic & Labour	High domestic & Grant	High domestic & Rateable value	Labour & Grant	Labour & Rateable value	Grant & Rateable value
Class I & II					0.360	0.229	0.222	0.117	0.115	−0.136
High domestic		−0.476	−0.418	−0.404				−0.261	−0.248	−0.374
Labour	0.331		0.305	0.305		0.123	0.137			0.305
Grant	0.164	0.288		0.153	0.159		0.166		0.135	
Rateable value	−0.018	−0.266	−0.102		−0.073	0.061		−0.074		

though the standard rate product does not reflect this. There does, therefore, appear to be an element of need in this factor as well. High social class composition is correlated with the domestic property values, but its relation with rates is reversed when they are taken together. The presence of a 'need' for lower rates seems most influential.

The operation of this factor is most intriguing as our indicators of public disposition showed such low relationships. This would argue against the notion of any direct electoral pressure, and in any case the number of people involved and the small number of wards normally covered by them makes this unlikely. A more likely explanation suggests itself if one looks at the general composition of the tax base. There is a strong inverse relation between the level of rate and the proportion of the tax base taken up by domestic property generally (-0.364). Clearly, the presence of high value property only reinforces this relationship. It seems likely that the relation between high property values and low rates results from an unwillingness on the part of councillors to tax such constituents, particularly where the incidence of the tax will be severe. Or it could be that they anticipate general electoral reactions from heavy taxation, an explanation which would fit with the very gradual increase in local rates which normally occurs. The widespread consensus about this view is apparent in the local authorities' acceptance of central grants and the recent introduction of the domestic element in the rate support grant.

As was observed earlier, the elasticity of the local rate is an important phenomenon which is probably influenced by anticipated reactions among councillors. The secular tendency for rates to increase in all local authorities confirms the flexibility of this tax when the pressures are strong enough. Here we have some evidence to suggest that councillors may act to reduce those pressures where the political consequences seem significant. There is also the widely established anti-tax attitude which operates at both levels of government. Labour governments are more ready to tax but even they experience inhibitions in certain circumstances.

The point of this analysis has been to confirm the value of this approach in examining the question of rates and the complementarity between rates and services. It is not possible to establish which decisions come first, though one suspects the revenue possibilities must dictate service spending. Perhaps a greater willingness to levy higher rates would alter the pattern of expenditure which we have found earlier. In fact our evidence shows that environmental factors operate to keep rates and spending in line, though this is not always efficiently done in any one authority.

11 Conclusions

The eight services outlined in Chapter 4 have now been analysed and their varying relationships to local needs, dispositions and resources have been explored. Similar relationships have also been shown to apply to the determination of rates, though this and substantive spending are obviously inter-related. While these analyses have usually involved only per capita spending they contain implicit assumptions about the quality of services. Particular expenditure decisions are not accounted for in this analysis, but the probability of local action is increased as the amounts spent increase. The analyses offer three broad returns. They tell us something about the model outlined in Chapter 3 and its suitability for understanding and explaining local politics. They also provide important findings about the operation of the system, highlighting some of the main parameters of local policy-making. Finally, and as a corollary of that, they indicate areas in which further research might profitably be undertaken.

Taken together the empirical analyses suggest that the model provides a valuable orientation. Allowing for shortcomings in the data, needs, dispositions and resources do show important, though varying relationships with the various local services. Even where the model shows its weakest relationships, valuable negative inferences may be drawn about policy-making in those service areas. Certainly it would seem that with better indicators, particularly of public and official disposition, the model would show sustained relevance across all services. In any event, as an heuristic device for orienting the observer to the many phenomena operating in the environment it is undoubtedly valuable.

Before looking at the collective implications of the analysis, each aspect of the model merits separate attention. Of the three major elements need displays the most consistent relationships across the varying services. No single environmental feature operates universally however, a factor of obvious importance when optimal local authority areas are being sought. The preoccupation with population size would seem from our results to involve serious overemphasis. Obviously, absolute service expenditures are greater in the larger authorities, but population size only affects our more comparative measure in the children's and police services. It may be that many features of administrative capacity and popular involvement are related to size, but the relationship is not reflected in per capita expenditure. The analysis here points to the need for a multivariate basis when defining local government areas. Age structure, social composition and a variety of physical characteristics are involved if one is to account for the likely pressures on any new local authority. It is also possible that evenly balanced populations create problems of policy decision and execution.

Of the indicators of need which were most relevant, the important distinction is between those of a personal and those of a physical character. On the personal side, social class provided a major underlying need which applied to almost all the services. At the same time, the age structure was of relevance for three services whose clientele fell into pronounced age groups. In physical terms, the condition of local housing had a pronounced impact, not only on council housing policies, but on other social services as well. The joint impact of both personal and physical characteristics raises interesting explanatory questions.

It is very relevant here that the most direct effect of need was observed in the case of education. This was entirely consistent with the compulsory nature of part of the service and the predominance of the compulsory segment in the whole field. Here it was obvious how need manifested itself independently of anything which the local authority might do, or any attitudes which it might adopt. Qualitative variations in provision obviously might occur, but schools must be provided. This situation does not apply in any other of our services. They vary in the degree of legislative obligation under which they are provided, and the supporting administrative directions are equally varied. (1) None, however, display the same control as education.

Where such compulsion is absent, the relative 'visibility' of objective need acquires greater importance. Whatever other factors are operating, the more visible the need the more likely that it will be met. Several of our services revealed that physical needs showed closer relationships with expenditure than might have been expected. It seems reasonable to attribute this to the visibility of such physical indicators when policies are being determined. Certainly the physical conditions of cities manifest themselves more clearly in most cases than do more personal factors. In addition, they are much more precisely quantifiable and this may be important to securing action by the government. This even shows itself in census data which are more informative about many physical characteristics of cities than about personal ones. One example of this is the absence of information about handicapped people and the consequent under-development of provision for them. Here the lack of knowledge about need is perhaps the major reason for non-provision.

A further possibility, bearing on our concept of disposition, is that physical needs have a more persuasive ring than personal ones. Though the evidence is slight, it does appear that councillors are happier in discussion of more concrete questions and in areas where results are likely to be detectable and measurable. Social problems in their more personal manifestations are much less easy to grasp and involve a great deal of subjective assessment.

Thus our data indicate that visibility is an important consideration. They also suggest that broad features of local authorities are of relevance in determining the levels of service to be adopted. This in itself is a characteristic of visibility. It is the broad social and economic characteristics which are immediately available from existing data, and detailed investigation of particular authorities confirms that they rely very much on such available data. Many other needs may exist but require independent research if they are to be discovered. This is beyond the capacity of most local authorities.

In spite of the impact of these rather general features the data showed

111

a distinct gap between services where the beneficiaries are an obvious and discrete section of the community and those which are more general. This was shown in the differences between the health services and the other personal social services, or between housing and education. Apart from visibility clear definition of the clientele being served may be an effective substitute for legal compulsion in a service. If the service is permissive and very general it is less likely to respond to need than where it is more specific. The local authority may need to be directed to clients rather more obviously than happens in some cases. Age categories are one obvious example in our data, but domestic standards and housing yardsticks could become equally rigorous.

These points about need, though analytically distinct, are very much bound up with the second aspect of our model, namely disposition. 'Visibility' is an essential ingredient to the development of disposition, enhancing the possibility of the varied aspects of disposition being brought into play. That is to say, it enhances the degree to which standards and beneficiaries are observable. It may also have an impact on the degree to which government action in any instance is regarded as legitimate.

Disposition itself was found to be related to all of our services, though interesting variations occurred. Councillor disposition was varied as between services, and our measures of officer and public disposition showed some relevance. The limitations of these latter factors seem almost certain to be a product of the poor indicators available, especially in the case of officials.

Councillor disposition measured in party terms was most relevant. It should be remembered here that party is seldom seen as having a bearing on local action, (2) and is often seen as an unnecessary and undesirable intrusion into local government. Each of these views may be perfectly tenable in normative terms, but our data suggest that they are an inaccurate reflection of the empirical position. Party was shown to be relevant and the degree of relevance varied precisely with our dispositional dimensions. Party was most engaged where two factors were present. As predicted, Labour councils were more active in services with a significant impact on the overall role of government. They were bigger spenders on the bigger services. In addition, they were more active where the service appeared to benefit sections of the community supporting them. Even where these two factors were less operative, there was a tendency for Labour to favour higher standards in the broadest sense. Our evidence suggests very clearly that party affects priorities established between services. At the same time, the data on grammar schools, especially when taken with earlier work on comprehensives, and the data on council rents, suggest that party may affect priorities within services as well.

Though the form of analysis involved here imposes limitations, this aspect of party impact is worth exploring further. Earlier, in Chapter 3, it was shown how party control related to the effectiveness of council operatio That analysis is expanded and elaborated in Table 11-1. This shows that a number of important local features are associated with the fact of a Labour majority. Business is expedited in terms of the length of council meetings. This is more remarkable when it is observed that Labour is also associatec

Table 11-1. Simple correlations between per cent Labour membership of the council and selected features of authority organisation

Authority organisation	Correlation
Average length of council meetings	-0.446
Number of sub-committees	0.195
Number of ad hoc committees	0.142
Items not approved by the council	-0.356
Items referred back by the council	-0.257
Whether questions were asked in council meetings	-0.181
Number of deputy and vice-chairmanships held by opposition parties	-0.230
Number of occasions in which mayoralty held by opposition parties	-0.269
Limitation of chairmanships which may be held by one individual	-0.121
Limitation on tenure of main committee chairmanship	0.110
Limitation on tenure of sub-committee chairmanships	0.179
Admission of press to committees other than Education	-0.013
Agenda papers available to press at least one clear day before council	-0.139
Press comment permitted before council meeting	-0.098
Public attendance at council meetings	-0.375

with more elaborate committee arrangements. The speed with which Labour councils deal in council with much more elaborate committee structures no doubt reflects the impact of party in such committees. Decisions taken in committee do not need to be given lengthy consideration in council as committees adhere to overall party policy.

This impression is echoed in the high inverse correlation between Labour control and items referred back or not approved. The formalisation of council approval is open to several interpretations but the most probable is that party ensures the 'right' recommendations from committees. Again this tendency of Labour councils is reinforced by the relative absence of any 'questions' in such authorities. This disregard for one of the cherished parliamentary defences against government control is indicative of party dominance. It may also reflect the greater accessibility of local officials to ordinary opposition council members, and the collective responsibility of

113

committees. It certainly means that much less public inquisition takes place when Labour controls.

The table provides further evidence of this. Four measures indicative of the degree of public information, both direct and indirect, show negative association with Labour control. Public attendance at council meetings is markedly lower, but in addition the possibility of press coverage is reduced. Documents are less available to the press and admission to meetings is more restricted under Labour control. However one views the role and performance of local newspapers such limitations certainly cannot help the process of public information.

Finally a series of other points emerge from the table, all bearing on the same general point. In patronage terms Labour is less generous to other parties. This may or may not have direct significance, but needs to be seen as part of a complex winner-take-all strategy. Though the data are not available here, one assumes this also extends to the election of Aldermen, which can of course influence the continuity of party control. This element of continuity is also reflected in longer tenure of committee chairmanships under Labour. While this could introduce an element of personal impact, the well-established caucus system probably makes it simply a vehicle for party control.

Although these figures related to only one year they indicate the very strong tendency for Labour councils to be more domineering in most senses of the term; at least, that is, in relation to opposition parties. When one looks at their relationship with officers the information becomes less definite. This is an important problem because tight and effective party control could lead to two alternative explanations of policy direction. On the one hand, it could mean that party has set up the necessary mechanics for implementing its own positions. On the other hand, it could mean that party creates the mechanisms but that they are simply an effective means of transforming official suggestions into effective policy. This is the key question in many areas of government and implicit normative attitudes towards the answer underlie many of the procedures of English local authorities.

Our analysis tells us something about this question, though it tends to be of a rather indirect nature. In one major sense it supports the first interpretation of party control. Where party was most related to service expenditure the relationship was entirely consistent with established party positions towards given services. The procedures which correlate with party control serve to strengthen the likelihood of such party policies being implemented.

This is not a final determination, however. It may be that procedural efficiency, which may have been established with party goals in mind, has been used by officers to implement policies with which they sympathise. The data available here only permit supposition for the moment. Measures of officer autonomy were used throughout the analysis and showed little relationship with any services. The interpretation of party control being adopted here suggests that processes are more subtle and that other measures may need to be sought. Assuming, as we did, that officers favour expansion of services and development of their own professional skills, it may be better to achieve this, not by becoming autonomous, which would be

114

at variance with many established norms, but by working with a party majority which shared similar views and would implement them. Such a notion requires detailed testing and officers in Conservative authorities would merit particularly close examination. Perhaps such authorities recruit different kinds of officer, or perhaps they have frustrated staff. Or it may be that officer impact is most reflected in more detailed aspects of services and that these need to be examined. The author has evidence from one county borough, however, which is controlled by an untypical Labour group on the evidence of our analysis. It displays the procedural characteristics outlined above as typical but does not use the resulting power to develop services. These remain under-developed and there is evidence of some officer frustration which would support the comments about officers favouring service expansion.(3)

Public impact on our services was usually small as an independent aspect of disposition. Much of this could be due to the particular measures being used which ignore participation by organised groups. It is widely accepted that local electoral variations are largely the product of national factors. (4) Our data tend to confirm this and may be interpreted as indicating the lack of relationship between turn-out and service performance. There may be electoral repercussions as a result of local factors, including service standards, but turn-out itself does not seem to be related. Given what is now known of party identification among voters, however, there does not seem much prospect of any other relationship either.

The related question of anticipated reactions among councillors affecting their service decisions has received some attention recently. (5) It is possible that councillors trim their policy decisions to their expectations of popular reaction, but our data suggest not very often. They indicate that each party does in fact follow a policy favourable to its basic traditional supporters. Anticipation is unnecessary if the parties follow policies coincidental with the interests of their respective voters.

Finally, the data about resources indicate the importance of this aspect of our model as well as suggesting certain important aspects of the central-local relationship. Finance has come to be accepted as the major limitation on government. Our services showed an important relationship with local resources, though it was the poor authorities who were the big spenders. This meant two things. In the first place, it meant considerable pressure on local resources with resultant heavy rates, as our measures showed. How equitable this is depends on the distribution of rateable value, though domestic rate-payers figured less prominently in these authorities. In spite of this, the rate as a source of revenue and the pattern of poor authorities mean that there is less redistribution of resources involved in this high expenditure. The less well-off pay higher rates to support the services which they require. This holds true in spite of the relative heterogeneity of English towns compared with American local governments. It is most interesting to see how the areas defined by the Royal Commission on Local Government for their new authorities alter this situation and spread more widely the burden presented by urban centres.

Against this feature of differential local hardship must be set the fact that these authorities are helped disproportionately by central government grants. The figure for rate deficiency grants used in our analysis showed this very clearly, especially where the more expensive services were concerned. Even if this form of grant does not create absolute parity as between rich and poor authorities, it does at least ease the burden on local rate-payers.(6)

The real element of redistribution in resource terms is effected by this central grant. In this respect it is also helped by the overall system of grants which enable these poorer authorities to achieve high levels of expenditure in costly services like education. These factors reinforce the Local Authority Associations' claim that central finance is an essential part of financing local services. Given the use of property as the major tax base, this seems the only way to ensure effective redistribution without re-drawing local boundaries. Any other consequences of this technique in the form of central dictation seem to be small. The local authorities which benefit are responding to local pressures and not to central controls. In addition, although it helps central finance does not obviate the need for higher local rates.

No doubt other resources are also significant but they could not be dealt with here. Land and labour are of obvious relevance to many services, as was noted earlier. However, they seem more likely to affect detailed aspects of most services rather than the broad outlines with which we have been concerned. Few services rely exclusively for their provision on these particular resources, while all require extensive finance. Indeed it is possible that finance can solve the labour problem for any particular locality, though obviously not nationally if shortages of staff are present. Land is a separate issue but probably has its main bearing on housing provision, at least among our selected services.

Altogether, the resource aspect of our model has something of the nature of a residual factor. Resources do not cause spending, even though some wealthy authorities are big spenders. They do however limit how far any authority can go. The pressures to spend have to be greater in order to go ahead in spite of rate implications. At the same time, Chapter 10 showed that this depended on the nature of the tax base. The advantage of the poorer authorities is that they have fewer domestic rate-payers who suffer disproportionately from high rates and who can effectively oppose their application. Though spared this particular opposition to high rates, there are obviously limits to the rate poundage an authority can apply. This has a clear effect on the levels of service which can be attained.

Each aspect of our model thus shows a clear and important relation to the varied local activities which have been considered. The major parameters affecting each service are clear from the analysis. Other factors will of course come into play but have to be seen in a context provided by the pattern of variables which has been displayed. Emphasis on individual roles in much political science writing has obscured the fact that individuals operate in a limiting environment. Choices are never unlimited and there are often tendencies at work which make for certain outcomes rather than others. This is not to take a determinist view. Our data leave much unexplained and, as was pointed out earlier, individual impact can be considerable in particular circumstances. It does show, however, that the individual who

Table 11-2. Simple correlations between per capita spending on the services and County Boroughs distributed by region

Expenditure per 1000 population on	South	Midlands	North-East	North-West
Welfare	0.258	—0.176	0.104	-0.185
Health	—0.082	—0.165	0.131	0.107
Children	—0.008	—0.040	0.042	0.003
Libraries	0.171	—0.248	0.012	0.058
Fire	—0.070	—0.233	—0.011	0.284
Police	0.163	—0.185	—0.265	0.269
Education	—0.228	0.128	0.257	—0.148
Local authority house building	—0.249	—0.109	0.194	0.153

responds to environmental pressures most closely is likely to win in many conflict situations, though not all. Nor does our data mean that all authorities behave uniformly. It simply means that there is a distinct probability that authorities which display the related patterns of needs, dispositions and resources which we have analysed will have appropriate service levels.

On this point it is worth considering some classificatory system for local authorities to see whether the data provide a basis for any systematic typology. This has been attempted by various people over a lengthy period, (7) and serves to focus attention when considering various aspects of local government. Perhaps the most obvious initial way of looking at this problem is to take a geographical division to see if that produces any pattern. Various subdivisions are possible, but to keep the number of county boroughs in each region reasonably high a four-fold classification has been applied in Table 11-2.

This indicates that a number of services vary between regions in interesting and perhaps important ways. Authorities in the South display a clear three-fold division among the services. Favourable patterns of spending are shown for welfare, libraries and police. Distinct negative correlations are shown for council housing and school spending, while the remaining services show negative though only small relationships. The Midland authorities reveal an equally clear, though more negative pattern. Only education shows a positive relationship and apart from the children's service the negative relationship is quite marked. The North-East shows much more positive relationships, only the police and fire services reversing this tendency. Education and housing are the region's strongest services. The

117

Table 11-3. Simple correlations between per capita spending on the services

	Welfare	Children	Health	Libraries	Fire	Police	Education	Housing
Welfare	1.000							
Children	0.296	1.000						
Health	0.494	0.456	1.000					
Libraries	0.224	0.037	0.211	1.000				
Fire	0.175	0.008	0.131	0.078	1.000			
Police	0.238	0.237	0.146	0.292	0.199	1.000		
Education	−0.030	0.282	0.136	−0.129	0.114	−0.201	1.000	
Housing	0.195	0.371	0.390	0.009	0.376	−0.017	0.431	1.000

North-West shows a similar strength of positive association but it is the fire and police services which show the most outstanding relationships.

Regional patterns do emerge therefore but this itself requires explanation. It could be that ideas travel geographically and that precepts are more obvious when they emerge in neighbouring authorities. It could be that inter-authority relationships are involved and that these must depend on geographical proximity. Very little work has been done on the diffusion of ideas to test such explanations. More probably, therefore, these patterns are related to the fact that the whole idea of distinct regions is based on the assumption of regional homogeneity, certainly in terms of demographic and socio-economic characteristics. The great relevance of these is clear in our analysis and can explain many of the relationships revealed in Table 11-2.

Perhaps some more sophisticated classification is possible. Our concern has been with the behaviour rather than the location of local authorities and it is there that important patterns may be found. The regularities of political activity are of major interest to the political scientist and county boroughs do reveal such regularities.

Before looking at the authorities themselves, the services deserve some comment. It was remarked earlier that education and housing are often seen as social services along with the more obvious traditional ones. Table 11-3 suggests that this is an oversimplification, and that the patterning of services treated here is quite complex. In terms of these simple correlations certain services do fall into distinct groups, but there are ones which are less strongly tied into a number of such groupings. The three traditional social services, children, health and welfare, are related, though welfare shows other attachments which mark it off, as one would expect from the earlier analysis. Housing relates closely to these three, but it is also coincident with fire service and educational spending. The latter is more weakly connected with the traditional social services, except for children, where a common clientele leave their mark. The fire service shows some moderate relationships with welfare and police, but its only major connection is with housing. Finally, the police and library services do form a group, though each displays several other relationships of almost equal order.

Given such imprecise groupings any classification of county boroughs becomes rather difficult. Table 11-4, however, shows that there is at least a principal three-fold division to be made. Roughly one quarter of all county boroughs either spend generously on most of the services, or spend very little on any of them. These two groups form the basis for extreme categories of a three-fold division. The former group favour maximisation of the scope of government and the latter minimal government action. Of those who fall in the middle positions it remains to be seen whether there are any distinguishing characteristics.

Examination of the patterns of spending by these authorities reveals a complex picture. No very distinct pattern of service emphasis emerges. Of the group spending above-average on only three services one observation is perhaps relevant. Eight of these spend above the average on education, the most expensive service of our group. This does not imply a commitment to government action of a broader kind, however, even though in five of those

119

Table 11-4. Pattern of per capita spending among County Boroughs on the services

Above median on	Number of County Boroughs	
8 services	2 ⎱	
7 "	6 ⎬	21
6 "	13 ⎰	
5 services	13 ⎱	
4 "	11 ⎬	43
3 "	19 ⎰	
2 services	4 ⎱	
1 "	8 ⎬	17
0 "	5 ⎰	

cases there is also high spending on housing. Commitment would suggest a move to develop more than one residual service, particularly as all of the remaining ones are relatively cheap. From our analysis it seems clear that the impact of need is felt in these two service areas but is not sufficient in other areas to persuade the authority to take action.

Examination of the remaining low spenders reveals another characteristic which is related to their general orientation. They show a distinct tendency to spend on the more traditional services such as fire and police. Where they do spend on a social service the rather deviant welfare case is the most common. As one would expect, these county boroughs do not show the sort of commitment which might spread, at any rate among our selected services.

Though neither of these tendencies is altogether general they both confirm the validity of treating this group as falling among the low spenders. An exception could be made for the five authorities which spend higher amounts on the two most expensive services. This implies heavy spending by government, but as has been suggested, is not reflected in other services.

A similar case can be developed for placing those county boroughs which spend above-average in five services with the group of general spenders. As one might expect at this level of service development no pattern is particularly clear. All services do relatively well, although police and education are developed in the fewest cases. In only one case, however, does the above-average expenditure pattern exclude both housing and education, making that authority's general commitment smaller in overall terms. In any event these are relatively big spenders and could go with our higher group.

This leaves only the small group of authorities who spend above-average amounts on four services. Once again the distribution among the services is very even, with the exception of education on which only three authorities fall in this category. Although housing is more developed than education, there is some reason here for assuming that the members of this group are like the first of those dealt with earlier (high spenders on three services). As in that case, this conclusion is supported by the emphasis on more traditional services being as high as that on social services. Indeed the fire service shows the most consistent high spending of all. There is thus a case for treating this group as low spenders, perhaps excepting the three boroughs with high educational spending.

The result of this analysis is to confirm the complexity of any classificatory scheme. Some of this is due to our having simply dichotomised the spending categories into high and low. A more refined breakdown would perhaps give better results, though the earlier correlation of service expenditures suggests not. Equally, the inclusion of other services, especially of a non-social-service kind, might help to show more clearly any division between the social services and others. This may be of great importance, as it has been shown to relate to party ideology fairly closely.

This rather unsatisfactory classificatory attempt does not detract from the importance of the relationships which were outlined earlier. Nor does it obscure the obvious research questions which those relationships suggest. Given that need is important in a number of cases, how is that need made apparent to the political decision-makers? Our data suggest that the public do not often transmit their needs in any direct way, for example through the electoral process. This leaves an obvious need for more information on the media of communication in this particular role. More particularly it raises the question of the precise role of voluntary organisations in this connection. The indicators used here failed to take account of this factor, and only the most general inferences could be drawn. The absence of work on this whole aspect of local politics is quite remarkable, given its recognised importance nationally. Perhaps it stems from the unwillingness to see local authorities as policy-making bodies which was commented on in Chapter 1.

A second major research area is that of the policy processes within the council. Obviously from our analysis, policy-makers can themselves operate to convert environmental needs into effective pressures for decision. More important is the traditional question about the roles of officers and councillors. Much more detailed analysis is necessary to determine their relative impact on policy. The analysis here suggested that councillors were most important, but this not only varied with the service but also left a question mark over the part played by officials. Evidence about the role of officials is obviously needed and more reliable indicators of their impact are required. It seems certain that they do play a prominent part in various ways, but whether it is uniform across services and how it varies if not are important questions.

Other less important matters are also raised. The legislative basis of many local services has obvious importance and great relevance for their autonomy. The whole question of central control perhaps merits further consideration in the light of local variation reported here. Do local authorities invoke central controls as an excuse for acting in certain ways which they themselves prefer? Do they vary in their capacity and willingness to defy central authority and, if so, what are the major characteristics involved? These questions were not touched by our analysis but are thrown into relief by it.

A further set of related questions concerns the basis and extent of local financing. This was dealt with in some detail but leaves many questions unanswered. Local attitudes to central funds were reasonably clear, but the whole process of rate determination and budgeting remains to be examined. The essence of our analysis was the determination of spending priorities and how this is done assumes great significance. There are now signs of more rational processes being introduced into local authority budgeting, but there is little general information about the present set-up or the criteria which are involved. Such gaps need to be filled.

It may be that our analysis raises as many questions as it answers. Certainly it seems to contain implications for any form of local reorganisation, particularly at the political level. In a field where there are very few general and well-tested relationships established it is difficult to lay down any common framework. The point of this work has been to establish some such relationships. At the same time as all county boroughs are different they also share many general characteristics. It is to these that our attention has been devoted. The differences, in terms of personalities and particular qualitative characteristics, are too often revealed.

122

Appendix A

SOURCES FOR ENGLISH COUNTY BOROUGH DATA

1. Welfare service statistics, 1965-6: Institute of Municipal Treasurers and Accountants and The Society of County Treasurers, December 1966.
2. Children's services statistics: Institute of Municipal Treasurers and Accountants and The Society of County Treasurers, December 1966.
3. Local health services statistics: Institute of Municipal Treasurers and Accountants and The Society of County Treasurers, December 1966.
4. Public library statistics, February 1966: Institute of Municipal Treasurers and Accountants and The Society of County Treasurers, December 1966.
5. Fire services statistics: Institute of Municipal Treasurers and Accountants and The Society of County Treasurers, December 1966.
6. Police force statistics: Institute of Municipal Treasurers and Accountants and The Society of County Treasurers, December 1966.
7. Housing statistics, 1965-6: Institute of Municipal Treasurers and Accountants, February 1967.
8. Education statistics: Institute of Municipal Treasurers and Accountants, February 1967.
9. C. A. Moser & Wolf Scott, **British towns** (London, Oliver & Boyd, 1961).
10. General Register Office, **Census 1961, England and Wales, County Reports** (London, H.M.S.O., 1965).
11. **Rates and Rateable Values in England and Wales, 1966-1967** (Ministry of Housing and Local Government and Welsh Office, H.M.S.O., undated).
12. **Municipal Yearbook, 1966.**
13. **The Registrar General's Statistical Review of England and Wales, 1964-1965** (London, H.M.S.O., undated).
14. Ministry of Education, **Education Statistics, 1965** (London, H.M.S.O., 1966).
15. Ministry of Housing and Local Government, **Management of Local Government**, vol. 5 (London, H.M.S.O., 1967).

VARIABLE USED

Variable number		Source
1	Borough population in thousands	10
2	Percentage of population in social classes I & II, 1951	9
3	Percentage of population in social classes IV & V, 1951	9
4	Percentage of population aged 0-4, 1961	10

Variable number		Source
5	Percentage of population aged 5-14, 1961	10
6	Percentage of population aged 65 and over, 1961	10
7	Percentage of occupied population aged 20-24 whose terminal education age was under 15, 1951	9
8	Percentage of population aged 15-25 attending full time at an educational establishment, 1951	9
9	Percentage of dwellings owner-occupied, 1961	10
10	Percentage of dwellings rented from the local authority, 1961	10
11	Percentage of households having exclusive use of four standard amenities, 1961	10
12	Percentage of council memberships held by Labour Party, average for 1963-6	12
13	Percentage turn-out at municipal elections, 1964	13
14	Percentage turn-out at municipal elections, 1965	13
15	Rate levied, 1965-6	11
16	Per capita rateable value, 1966-7	11
17	Percentage of rateable value which was domestic property, 1966-7	11
18	Percentage of domestic rateable value in units over £100 in value, 1966-7	11
19	Percentage rate deficiency grant, 1966-7	11
20	Density of population per acre, 1965-6	1
21	Percentage of population living above 1 and 1/2 people per room, 1951	10
22	Percentage of population living above 1 and 1/2 people per room, 1961	10
23	Average length of council meetings	15
24	Number of main committees	15
25	Number of sub-committees	15
26	Total number of ad hoc committees which met at least once in the last year	15
27	Number of committee recommendations not approved in last twelve months	15
28	Number of committee recommendations referred back in last twelve months	15
29	Whether 'questions' were asked in the last three council meetings	15
30	Percentage of deputy chairmanships and vice-chairmanships not held by majority party	15
31	Percentage of mayors in last ten years not from majority party	15
32	Whether or not there is a limit on the tenure of the chair of the main committees	15

Variable number		Source
33	Whether the press is admitted to any committees other than education	15
34	Whether agenda papers are made available to the press at least one clear day before council meetings	15
35	Whether the press is permitted to comment on these before council meetings	15
36	Approximate average public attendance at council meetings	15
37	Number of sheets of paper circulated to councillors in a typical month	15
38	Whether organisation has either an Organisation and Methods officer or a work study organisation	15
39	Whether authority has employed either an Organisation and Methods officer or a work study consultant in last five years.	15
40	Number of separate departments in the local authority	15
41	Expenditure on welfare services per 1000 population, 1965-6	1
42	Expenditure on children's services per 1000 population, 1965-6	2
43	Expenditure on local health services per 1000 population, 1965-6	3
44	Expenditure on public libraries per 1000 population, 1965-6	4
45	Books issued per head of population, 1965-6	12
46	Expenditure on fire service per 1000 population, 1965-6	5
47	Rateable value of property per fireman, 1965-6	5 and 11
48	Expenditure on police service per 1000 population, 1965-6	6
49	Population per policeman, 1965-6	6
50	Percentage of new houses built by council, 1945-58	9
51	Expenditure on education per 1000 population, 1965-6	8
52	Percentage of secondary school places taken up by grammar schools	14

Appendix B

CORRELATION MATRIX OF VARIABLES USED

Variable number	1	2	3	4	5	6	7
1	1.000	−0.083	−0.010	0.123	0.010	−0.166	0.136
2		1.000	−0.787	−0.531	−0.629	0.650	−0.570
3			1.000	0.510	0.644	−0.537	0.536
4				1.000	0.732	−0.726	0.284
5					1.000	−0.718	0.406
6						1.000	−0.502
7							1.000

Variable number	8	9	10	11	12	13	14
1	−0.131	−0.180	0.101	−0.089	0.080	−0.420	−0.336
2	0.766	0.600	−0.557	0.588	−0.779	0.280	0.427
3	−0.570	−0.535	0.372	−0.493	0.707	−0.240	−0.402
4	−0.498	−0.378	0.369	−0.134	0.432	−0.234	−0.268
5	−0.646	−0.484	0.479	−0.201	0.550	−0.175	−0.277
6	0.676	0.360	−0.486	0.174	−0.534	0.359	−0.424
7	−0.797	−0.448	0.342	−0.334	0.424	−0.482	−0.544
8	1.000	0.516	−0.500	0.443	−0.571	0.389	0.473
9		1.000	−0.729	0.286	−0.483	0.355	0.446
10			1.000	−0.010	0.371	−0.217	−0.296
11				1.000	−0.533	0.007	0.198
12					1.000	−0.149	−0.363
13						1.000	0.887
14							1.000

Variable number	15	16	17	18	19	20	21
1	0.184	0.064	−0.233	0.040	−0.172	0.423	0.129
2	−0.308	0.452	0.309	0.810	−0.434	−0.350	−0.544
3	0.308	−0.538	−0.440	−0.641	0.545	0.302	0.563
4	0.147	−0.335	−0.305	−0.528	0.344	0.368	0.437
5	0.197	−0.461	−0.333	−0.620	0.380	0.376	0.491
6	−0.277	0.360	0.526	0.662	−0.264	−0.345	−0.449
7	0.106	−0.371	−0.454	−0.521	0.174	0.326	0.412
8	−0.203	0.432	0.516	0.721	−0.296	−0.369	−0.480
9	−0.151	0.206	0.454	0.402	−0.105	−0.437	−0.616
10	0.074	−0.134	−0.492	−0.464	0.009	0.133	0.419
11	−0.454	0.357	0.450	0.526	−0.452	−0.161	0.172
12	0.441	−0.445	−0.523	−0.682	0.429	0.289	0.447
13	0.080	−0.070	0.236	0.120	0.136	−0.412	−0.346
14	−0.059	0.065	0.310	0.288	−0.022	−0.411	−0.394

Variable number	22	23	24	25	26	27	28
1	0.313	0.138	0.309	0.206	0.082	−0.190	−0.159
2	−0.483	0.472	−0.001	−0.071	−0.127	0.231	0.167
3	0.466	−0.450	0.026	0.163	0.076	−0.205	−0.142
4	0.444	−0.332	0.010	0.114	0.075	−0.166	−0.153
5	0.433	−0.498	−0.104	0.047	−0.058	−0.290	−0.186
6	−0.427	0.386	−0.122	−0.059	−0.091	0.280	0.233
7	0.366	−0.256	−0.000	−0.013	−0.170	−0.106	−0.082
8	−0.463	0.406	0.054	−0.006	0.020	0.220	0.179
9	−0.603	0.343	0.123	0.013	−0.156	0.178	0.188
10	0.399	−0.270	−0.023	−0.109	0.188	−0.079	−0.140
11	−0.207	0.186	−0.064	−0.106	−0.029	0.229	0.115
12	0.376	−0.446	0.045	0.195	0.142	−0.356	−0.257
13	−0.416	0.028	−0.091	−0.176	0.078	−0.031	0.021
14	−0.450	0.123	−0.110	−0.078	0.064	0.049	0.091

Variable number	29	30	31	32	33	34	35
1	−0.011	0.158	0.033	−0.063	−0.022	−0.013	−0.078
2	0.205	0.188	0.106	0.092	0.016	0.021	0.134
3	−0.172	−0.136	−0.162	0.054	0.079	0.033	−0.218
4	−0.093	−0.164	−0.034	−0.150	−0.051	−0.073	−0.129
5	−0.115	−0.292	−0.047	−0.074	0.031	−0.015	−0.211
6	0.248	0.370	0.023	0.112	0.105	0.118	0.139
7	−0.087	−0.162	0.007	−0.020	−0.005	0.131	−0.054
8	0.124	0.165	−0.029	0.082	0.020	−0.025	0.132
9	0.084	0.076	0.122	0.018	−0.004	0.118	0.110
10	−0.223	−0.090	0.015	−0.015	−0.077	−0.092	−0.050
11	−0.090	−0.096	−0.073	0.176	−0.119	−0.150	0.070
12	−0.181	−0.230	−0.269	−0.121	−0.013	−0.139	−0.098
13	0.026	0.051	−0.056	0.102	0.039	−0.023	−0.100
14	0.019	0.102	−0.042	0.199	0.000	−0.042	−0.074

Variable number	36	37	38	39	40	41	42
1	0.192	0.097	0.030	−0.038	0.326	−0.078	0.338
2	0.456	0.044	0.014	−0.161	0.056	0.022	−0.375
3	−0.379	−0.053	−0.107	0.025	−0.110	0.006	0.237
4	−0.245	0.142	−0.083	0.022	−0.043	−0.170	0.188
5	−0.355	0.038	−0.140	0.105	−0.228	−0.189	0.205
6	0.225	−0.138	0.009	−0.083	0.029	0.204	−0.227
7	−0.267	−0.027	−0.181	0.065	−0.144	−0.186	0.183
8	0.328	0.006	−0.010	−0.185	0.082	0.252	−0.255
9	0.410	0.190	0.166	−0.060	0.227	−0.085	−0.248
10	−0.296	−0.183	−0.126	0.183	−0.189	−0.048	0.075
11	0.296	0.030	−0.146	−0.091	−0.119	−0.200	−0.348
12	0.375	0.106	0.055	0.014	0.089	0.007	0.314
13	0.047	−0.028	0.175	0.052	0.044	0.182	−0.236
14	0.159	−0.013	0.180	0.141	0.067	0.168	−0.233

Variable number	43	44	45	46	47	48	49
1	0.111	0.101	−0.064	−0.234	0.179	0.398	−0.158
2	−0.282	0.133	0.499	−0.325	0.371	0.189	−0.138
3	0.255	−0.070	−0.344	0.497	−0.511	0.011	−0.094
4	0.146	−0.025	−0.111	0.199	−0.347	−0.143	0.164
5	0.010	−0.123	−0.051	0.270	−0.421	−0.124	0.025
6	−0.133	0.166	−0.030	0.116	0.202	0.212	−0.220
7	0.110	−0.129	0.016	0.085	−0.036	−0.088	0.125
8	−0.111	0.220	0.077	−0.145	0.212	0.187	−0.214
9	−0.209	−0.077	0.349	−0.336	0.130	−0.004	−0.064
10	0.053	−0.017	−0.251	0.221	0.007	−0.271	0.301
11	−0.381	0.066	0.393	−0.259	0.397	−0.038	0.039
12	0.330	−0.056	−0.355	0.239	−0.405	−0.226	0.134
13	−0.026	0.116	−0.009	0.047	−0.247	−0.110	−0.063
14	−0.056	0.222	0.058	−0.012	−0.084	−0.027	−0.129

Variable number	50	51	52
1	0.028	0.074	−0.119
2	−0.806	−0.462	0.302
3	0.652	0.420	−0.212
4	0.358	0.578	−0.215
5	0.458	0.630	−0.254
6	−0.426	−0.746	0.259
7	0.325	0.292	−0.461
8	−0.494	−0.489	0.426
9	−0.543	−0.203	0.242
10	0.494	0.353	−0.208
11	−0.597	−0.253	0.065
12	−0.670	0.522	−0.180
13	−0.099	−0.038	0.310
14	−0.239	−0.201	0.254

Variable number	15	16	17	18	19	20	21
15	1.000	−0.396	−0.364	−0.523	0.410	0.085	0.080
16		1.000	0.069	0.676	−0.788	−0.066	−0.336
17			1.000	0.648	−0.008	−0.212	−0.237
18				1.000	−0.557	−0.208	−0.388
19					1.000	0.006	0.325
20						1.000	0.458
21							1.000

Variable number	22	23	24	25	26	27	28
15	0.125	−0.181	0.013	0.013	0.168	−0.384	−0.265
16	−0.254	0.521	0.111	−0.039	0.004	0.307	0.165
17	−0.241	0.234	−0.102	0.096	−0.083	0.197	0.140
18	−0.341	0.493	0.100	0.037	−0.016	0.354	0.247
19	0.270	−0.364	−0.060	0.059	0.056	−0.159	0.006
20	0.554	0.046	0.304	0.073	0.027	−0.142	−0.190
21	0.912	−0.093	0.012	0.147	0.252	−0.119	−0.028
22	1.000	−0.307	−0.052	0.209	0.314	−0.058	−0.009
23		1.000	0.161	0.018	−0.025	0.465	0.341
24			1.000	0.334	0.339	0.028	0.032
25				1.000	0.223	0.044	0.043
26					1.000	−0.053	−0.100
27						1.000	0.713
28							1.000

Variable number	29	30	31	32	33	34	35
15	−0.132	0.095	−0.010	−0.051	−0.036	−0.129	−0.004
16	0.183	0.234	0.111	−0.002	−0.054	−0.074	0.141
17	0.224	0.120	−0.042	0.050	0.041	0.135	0.109
18	0.253	0.184	0.015	0.075	0.036	0.042	0.092
19	−0.095	−0.044	−0.108	−0.052	0.047	0.164	−0.274

Variable number	29	30	31	32	33	34	35
20	−0.013	−0.094	−0.127	−0.038	0.019	−0.080	−0.014
21	−0.198	−0.176	−0.290	−0.080	0.173	−0.151	−0.224
22	−0.193	−0.065	−0.189	−0.152	0.181	−0.180	−0.227
23	0.319	0.240	0.243	−0.016	−0.056	0.154	0.171
24	0.072	0.056	0.064	−0.184	−0.011	−0.002	−0.125
25	−0.057	0.068	−0.140	−0.166	0.288	0.042	0.042
26	−0.117	0.000	−0.081	−0.132	0.077	−0.441	0.071
27	0.138	0.036	0.189	0.045	0.248	0.020	−0.091
28	0.051	−0.011	0.111	−0.014	0.239	−0.072	−0.322

Variable number	36	37	38	39	40	41	42
15	−0.138	−0.049	−0.021	−0.009	0.014	0.213	0.194
16	0.313	0.131	−0.018	0.057	0.068	0.048	−0.014
17	0.407	0.080	0.066	−0.044	0.040	−0.107	−0.383
18	0.488	0.157	0.041	−0.044	0.077	0.110	−0.221
19	−0.230	−0.016	−0.055	−0.012	−0.062	0.109	0.073
20	−0.077	−0.044	0.012	−0.065	−0.102	−0.042	0.453
21	−0.338	0.046	−0.066	0.195	−0.067	−0.098	0.230
22	−0.278	0.121	−0.024	0.137	−0.004	−0.114	0.257
23	0.489	0.111	0.004	0.071	0.072	−0.075	−0.151
24	0.278	0.448	0.096	−0.057	0.576	0.089	0.122
25	0.200	0.286	0.157	0.196	0.446	−0.083	0.216
26	0.223	0.222	0.245	0.097	0.403	0.187	0.003
27	0.218	0.139	−0.011	0.095	−0.071	−0.121	−0.122
28	0.160	0.163	−0.121	0.049	−0.098	−0.088	−0.048

Variable number	43	44	45	46	47	48	49
15	0.389	0.000	−0.057	0.132	−0.372	0.143	−0.199
16	−0.105	0.232	0.069	−0.198	0.580	0.224	−0.000
17	−0.310	−0.076	0.399	−0.208	0.102	0.080	−0.121

Variable number	43	44	45	46	47	48	49
18	−0.225	0.237	0.309	−0.272	0.508	0.290	−0.134
19	0.245	−0.049	−0.132	0.344	−0.682	−0.142	−0.033
20	0.215	0.010	−0.164	0.059	−0.059	0.266	−0.193
21	0.147	0.011	−0.229	0.259	−0.256	−0.052	0.024
22	0.182	0.076	−0.210	0.158	−0.105	0.023	0.033
23	−0.190	0.158	0.175	−0.222	0.306	0.138	−0.021
24	0.155	−0.052	0.074	−0.147	0.116	0.053	0.040
25	0.158	−0.086	−0.134	−0.030	−0.152	0.046	−0.081
26	0.261	0.035	−0.139	0.041	0.027	−0.007	−0.013
27	−0.265	0.128	−0.047	−0.202	0.300	−0.186	0.292
28	−0.159	0.189	−0.061	−0.256	0.198	−0.159	0.166

Variable number	50	51	52
15	0.430	0.493	0.153
16	−0.398	−0.269	0.061
17	−0.625	−0.462	0.270
18	−0.695	−0.580	0.196
19	0.464	0.319	0.106
20	0.278	0.180	−0.351
21	0.418	0.259	−0.120
22	0.437	0.267	−0.081
23	−0.437	−0.310	0.190
24	−0.103	0.069	0.127
25	0.066	−0.080	0.077
26	0.791	0.022	0.196
27	−0.323	−0.260	0.100
28	−0.097	−0.162	0.124

Variable number	29	30	31	32	33	34	35
29	1.000	0.094	0.176	0.004	−0.084	0.176	0.126
30		1.000	0.330	0.080	−0.018	0.116	0.106
31			1.000	0.004	−0.026	0.125	0.131
32				1.000	−0.135	0.154	−0.017
33					1.000	0.034	−0.243
34						1.000	0.000
35							1.000

Variable number	36	37	38	39	40	41	42
29	0.144	0.066	−0.043	−0.041	0.043	0.096	0.041
30	−0.061	−0.153	−0.146	0.138	0.108	0.232	0.144
31	0.048	−0.041	0.111	0.161	0.073	0.049	0.084
32	−0.016	−0.199	−0.122	−0.124	−0.179	0.076	0.041
33	0.025	0.018	0.049	0.172	0.063	0.035	0.045
34	0.047	−0.073	−0.161	−0.002	−0.043	0.031	0.010
35	0.005	−0.151	−0.161	−0.169	−0.163	−0.021	−0.108
36	1.000	0.256	0.243	0.019	0.315	0.033	−0.226
37		1.000	0.021	0.024	0.378	−0.266	−0.107
38			1.000	0.082	0.359	0.003	0.146
39				1.000	0.062	0.072	0.018
40					1.000	0.194	0.118
41						1.000	0.296
42							1.000

Variable number	43	44	45	46	47	48	49
29	−0.195	0.053	0.131	0.034	0.033	0.218	−0.103
30	0.179	0.182	−0.062	0.064	−0.051	0.146	−0.131
31	0.021	0.064	−0.004	−0.139	0.259	−0.028	0.036
32	−0.047	0.091	−0.102	0.140	−0.034	0.159	−0.208
33	0.020	0.038	−0.104	0.108	−0.142	0.145	−0.131

Variable number	43	44	45	46	47	48	49
34	−0.131	−0.066	−0.011	0.024	−0.007	0.006	0.069
35	−0.021	−0.224	−0.006	−0.200	0.166	−0.068	−0.001
36	−0.024	0.077	0.470	−0.337	0.221	0.276	−0.188
37	−0.105	0.175	0.257	−0.207	0.153	−0.102	0.212
38	0.121	0.038	0.067	−0.163	0.086	−0.073	0.042
39	0.022	−0.011	−0.181	0.162	0.045	−0.006	0.022
40	0.157	−0.055	−0.058	−0.132	0.047	−0.005	0.098
41	0.494	0.224	−0.213	0.175	−0.044	0.238	−0.193
42	0.456	0.037	−0.393	0.008	−0.038	0.237	−0.236

Variable number	50	51	52
29	−0.240	−0.134	−0.007
30	−0.117	−0.267	0.094
31	−0.109	−0.004	0.057
32	−0.130	−0.147	−0.137
33	0.074	−0.044	0.065
34	−0.104	−0.106	0.121
35	−0.104	−0.243	−0.107
36	−0.393	−0.187	0.007
37	−0.213	0.144	0.201
38	−0.030	−0.011	0.012
39	0.142	−0.047	0.105
40	−0.163	−0.025	0.123
41	0.195	−0.030	0.047
42	0.371	0.282	−0.231

Variable number	43	44	45	46	47	48	49
43	1.000	0.211	−0.232	0.131	−0.171	0.146	−0.147
44		1.000	0.017	0.078	0.106	0.292	−0.212
45			1.000	−0.163	0.050	0.138	−0.163
46				1.000	−0.625	0.199	−0.287
47					1.000	−0.008	0.273
48						1.000	−0.814
49							1.000

Variable number	50	51	52
43	0.390	0.136	−0.124
44	0.009	−0.129	0.098
45	−0.514	0.022	0.055
46	0.376	0.114	−0.123
47	−0.371	−0.257	0.124
48	−0.017	−0.201	0.038
49	−0.116	0.186	−0.053
50	1.000	0.431	−0.084
51		1.000	−0.148
52			1.000

Appendix C

THE STATISTICAL METHOD

The two measures used here to measure the relationships between county borough expenditures and needs, dispositions and resources, are the simple and partial correlation coefficient.

The simple correlation coefficient measures the degree of association between two variables. It may range in value from +1.000, which indicates a perfect positive relationship, to −1.000, which indicates a perfect negative relationship. Coefficients at or near to zero indicate the absence of a relationship between the two variables. Such coefficients are always comparable and a higher coefficient always indicates a closer association than a smaller one.

These simple correlation coefficients establish the presence or absence of relationships between two variables, but do not permit assumptions about causal relationships. It may be that a relationship between any two variables is a spurious one because of some intervening variable. A close relationship between two variables may be caused by their common relation to a third variable.

In order to deal with this problem the partial correlation coefficient is used. This measure shows the degree of relationship between two variables when the effect of one or more intervening variables is controlled. Like the simple coefficients these may also range from 1.000 for perfect positive association to −1.000 for perfect negative association. The size of the coefficient indicates the strength of relationship in the controlled conditions.

Neither of these measures establishes the existence of an explanatory relationship. Association must not be confused with causation. The partial correlation does, however, take the analysis closer to a causal one. It establishes association in specified and controlled circumstances. Any claim to explanation must rest, however, on the model being proposed and on the quality of the indicators used to illustrate it.

136

Notes to the Text

Chapter 1   APPROACHES TO THE COMMUNITY, pp. 1-10

1   The political interest is apparent in the recent series of government
     reports: the Mallaby (Committee on the Staffing of Local Government)
     Report, **Staffing of Local Government** (London, 1967); the Maud (Com-
     mittee on the Management of Local Government) Report, **Management
     of Local Government** (London, 1967); and the Redcliffe-Maud Report
     (Royal Commission on Local Government in England, 1966-9)
     (London, 1969). The academic interest is apparent in the extensive
     series of studies now being made with grants from the Social Science
     Research Council. Among the cities in which such work is being done
     are: Aberdeen, Birmingham, Dundee, Glasgow, Liverpool, Newcastle and
     Sheffield.
2   In addition to the research cited in note 1 there is also the substantial
     work done for the Royal Commission : Research Studies, vols. 1-10
     (London, 1968-9) and volume III of the Report, Research Appendices
     (London, 1969).
3   The political parties have carried out some studies, but more prominent
     are the local authority associations, and the professional bodies such as
     the Institute of Municipal Treasurers and Accountants and the Royal
     Institute of Public Administration.
4   The nearest to this approach are probably J. M. Lee, **Social leaders and
     public persons** (London, 1963) and A. H. Birch, **Small town politics**
     (London, 1959).
5   See for example, W. A. Robson, **Local government in crisis** (London,
     1966).
6   Maud Report, pp. 78-82.
7   W. O. Hart, **Introduction** to the law of local government and administra-
     tion, 8th edn. (London, 1969)
8   Gerald Rhodes, **Town government in South East England** (London, 1967),
     chap. 6 especially.
9   Robson, **Local government in crisis**, especially chap. X.
10   Ibid. See for example p. 61.
11   Ibid. p. 67.
12   Ibid. p. 62.
13   For example, L. J. Sharpe, A metropolis votes (London, 1962) and
     J. G. Bulpitt, **Party politics in English local government** (London, 1967).
14   Royal Institute of Public Administration, **New sources of local revenue**
     (London, 1956).
15   **Report of the Allen Committee of Inquiry into the Impact of Rates on
     Households,** Cmnd. 2582 (London, 1965).
16   Apart from the Hicks' attempts to do this during the war, J. R. & U. K.
     Hicks, **Standards of local expenditure** (London, 1943).

17 For one treatment of the question of 'anticipated reactions' in local government see R. G. Gregory, 'Local elections and the "role of anticipated reactions" ', Political Studies, XVII, 1 (March 1969), though his response on rates is weaker than that on certain other issues.

18 Examples would include: Birkenhead, Bury, South Shields and West Hartlepool.

19 For an interesting treatment of this question and the general notion of territorial justice, see B. P. Davies, Social needs and resources in local services (London, 1968).

20 Efforts have been made (for example in the Royal Commission Research Studies) but the results are inconclusive, in part because of the restricted range of variables used, which is the essence of the comments already made on the study of local government.

21 Report of the Local Government Boundary Commission (London, 1948).

22 Maud Report, vol. 3.

23 W. J. M. Mackenzie, Theories of local government (London, 1961).

24 L. J. Sharpe, Why local democracy?, Fabian Tract 361 (London, 1965).

25 Mackenzie, Theories of local government, p. 5.

26 The literature on this topic spans a considerable time period and the arguments are summarised in a number of places, for example Nelson W. Polsby, Community power and political theory (New Haven, 1963).

27 See for example Delbert C. Miller, 'Decision making cliques in community power structures', American Journal of Sociology (1957).

28 See for example M. Stacey, Tradition and change (London, 1960). Even where a more total approach has been adopted it has not been concerned with the outputs of the political system.

29 James Q. Wilson, 'Problems in the study of urban politics', in Essays in political science, ed. Edward H. Buehrig (Bloomington, 1966).

30 James Q. Wilson (ed.), City politics and public policy (New York, 1968).

31 Bulpitt, Party politics in English local government, does this, but only in terms of patronage in any detail. He has subsequently written as though party had little relevance for local policy, in 'Do local elections matter?', New Society, 9 May 1968.

32 C. A. Moser & Wolf Scott, British towns (London, 1961).

33 Notice the central concern with size in the more extensive Royal Commission Research Studies, cited in the Select Bibliography.

34 See the discussion of non-decisions in Peter Bachrach and Morton S. Baratz, 'Decisions and non-decisions: an analytical framework', American Political Science Review, vol. 57 (1963).

35 Reports of the Central Advisory Council on Education published in 'Crowther' (1959), 'Newsom' (1963) and 'Plowden' (1967).

36 Educational priority areas were designated recently in certain cities as areas of special educational need, though the criteria used were somewhat crude and the physical definitions rather obscure.

37 Peter H. Rossi, 'Theory, research and practice in community organisation', in Social science and community action, ed. Charles R. Adrian (East Lansing, 1960).

38 Rossi, ibid. p. 21.

39   Robert R. Alford, 'The comparative study of urban politics', in Urban
      research and policy planning, ed. Leo F. Schnore & Henry Fagin (San
      Francisco, 1967).

Chapter 2   VARIATIONS BETWEEN COUNTY BOROUGHS, pp. 11-20

1   Robson, Local government in crisis.
2   L. P. Green, Provincial metropolis (London, 1959), p. 156
3   Royal Commission on Local Government, para. 100.
4   J. A. G. Griffith, Central departments and local authorities (London,
      1966), pp. 528-9.
5   Robson, Local government in crisis, p. 149.
6   R.I.P.A., New sources of local revenue, p. 16.
7   Griffith, Central departments and local authorities, p. 511.
8   For a comment on the varied capability of central departments,
      see ibid. passim.
9   Royal Commission on Local Government, especially chap. 3.
10   See below chap. 4.
11   Julia Parker, Local health and welfare services (London, 1965).
12   Elizabeth Layton, Building by local authorities (London, 1961).
13   Department of Education and Science, Circular 10/65 (London, 1965)
14   Circular 10/65 outlined very precise schemes and asked for very
      specific proposals from local authorities.
15   See for example Royal Commission on Local Government, Research
      Study no. 3, Economies of Scale in Local Government Services (London,
      1968).
16   Robson, Local government in crisis, p. 61.
17   The rate deficiency grant was designed to give additional support to
      local authorities with inadequate sources of local revenue in relation
      to national standards.
18   Noel T. Boaden & Robert R. Alford, 'Sources of diversity in English
      local government decisions', Public Administration (Summer 1969).

Chapter 3   A MODEL OF THE LOCAL POLITICAL SYSTEM, pp. 21-35

1   The rate deficiency grant being considered here included an element
      allowing for numbers of very young children, of school-age children
      and old people, as well as for road mileages, considered to be indica-
      tive of certain needs
2   Lewis Froman Jr, 'An analysis of public policies in cities', Journal of
      Politics, vol. 29 (1967), presents a division between areal and segmen-
      tal policies analogous to that being adopted here.
3   Report of the Committee on Local Authority and Allied Personal Social
      Services (London, 1968).
4   Oliver P. Williams, Harold Herman, Charles S. Liebman & Thomas R.
      Dye, Suburban differences and metropolitan policies: a Philadelphia
      story (Philadelphia, 1965), explore this feature of the Philadelphia
      metropolitan area.

5   Robert K. Merton, **Social theory and social structure** (Glencoe, 1949), develops the notion of 'local' and 'cosmopolitan' orientations which are reflected in attitudes about the locality.
6   James S. Coleman, **Community conflict** (Glencoe, 1957).
7   Robert E. Agger, Daniel Goldrich & Bert E. Swanson, **The rulers and the ruled** (New York, 1964), pp. 6-14.
8   See, for example, Karl A. Bosworth, 'The manager is a politician', **Public Administration Review**, vol. 18 (1958).
9   Arthur Skeffington, **People and planning** (London, 1969).
10 See **Report of the Working Party on Social Workers in the Local Authority Health and Welfare Services** (London, 1959).
11 On **Staffing of Local Government.**
12 Layton, **Building by local authorities.**
13 Williams et al., **Suburban differences and metropolitan policies.**
14 Ibid.
15 Dennis J. Palumbro & Oliver P. Williams, 'Predictors of public policy: the case of local public health', **Urban Affairs Quarterly**, II, 4 (June 1967).
16 See for example John C. Bollens (ed.), **Exploring the metropolitan community** (Berkeley, 1961).
17 Williams et al., **Suburban differences and metropolitan policies**, chap. 4.
18 J. B. Cullingworth, 'The measurement of housing need', **British Journal of Sociology**, IX, 4 (Dec. 1958).
19 Many issues which are salient for business men are regional or national in scope and this is reinforced by absentee ownership. Small business owners may, however, be disproportionately represented on local councils and may derive benefits in terms of low rates or planning knowledge.
20 See 'Children in care', **New Society**, 2 May 1968.
21 Gabriel A. Almond & Sidney Verba, **The civic culture** (Princeton, 1963).
22 Rate deficiency grants were payable to those authorities whose penny rate product fell below the 'standard product' for their area. The latter is the sum having the same proportion to the total national 1d. rate product as the population does to the national population.
23 Lawrence Boyle, **Equalisation and the future of local government finance** (London, 1966).

Chapter 4   THE SERVICES, pp. 36-44

1   Much work on American States has adopted a very similar framework for analysis: see for example, Thomas R. Dye, **Politics, economics, and the public** (Chicago, 1966).
2   Alford, 'The comparative study of urban politics'.
3   Robert C. Wood, **1400 governments** (New York, 1964), p. 40.
4   Aaron Wildavsky, **Politics of the budgetary process** (Boston, 1964).
5   Bollens, **Exploring the metropolitan community.**
6   Davies, **Social needs and resources,** pp. 43-4, 20.
7   Ibid. p. 43

8   Vincent Ostrom, Charles M. Tiebout & Robert Warren, 'The organisa-
        tion of government in metropolitan areas: a theoretical inquiry',
        American Political Science Review, LV, 4 (Dec. 1961).
9   Davies, **Social needs and resources,** pp. 70, 81.
10   Maud Report, vol. 3, p. 5.
11   Ibid. p. 43.
12   Bulpitt, **Party politics in English local government.**
13   This point is made in L. J. Sharpe (ed.), **Voting in cities** (London, 1967).

Chapter 5   EDUCATION, pp. 45-58

1   See above p. 42
2   See above p. 8
3   The Education Act 1944 says that the duty of the Secretary of State
        'Shall be to promote the education of the people of England and Wales
        and the progressive development of institutions devoted to that purpose,
        and to secure the effective execution by local authorities, under his
        control and direction, of the national policy for providing a varied and
        comprehensive educational service in every area'.
4   **The Times** (London), 21 August 1968.
5   F. Bealey & D. J. Bartholemew, 'The local elections in Newcastle-under-
        Lyme, May 1968', **British Journal of Sociology,** XIII, 3 & 4 (1962)
6   Circular 10/65.
7   Boaden and Alford, 'Sources of diversity in English local government
        decisions'.
8   For a review of the ambivalence shown by Labour politicians, see
        M. H. Parkinson, **The Labour Party and the organisation of secondary
        education, 1918-65** (London, 1970).
9   Maud Report, vol, 3, pp. 44, 50-1, 56.
10   Ibid. pp. 26-7.
11   Alford, 'The comparative study of urban politics'.
12   **The Times,** 21 August 1968.
13   See Parkinson, **Labour Party and secondary education.**
14   R. Batley, H. Parris & O. O'Brien, **Going comprehensive** (London, 1970).
15   Boaden & Alford, 'Sources of diversity in English local government
        decisions'.

Chapter 6   HOUSING, pp. 59-70

1   The origins of local authority housing activity are to be found in the
        major cities in the 1860s and 1870s, though building did not reach any
        appreciable level until the latter part of the century.
2   National Board for Prices and Incomes, Report no. 62: **Increases in
        Rents of Local Authority Housing** (London, 1968).
3   Boaden & Alford, 'Sources of diversity in English local government
        decisions'.
4   P.I.B. Report, para. 2.
5   Ibid. para. 5.

6   Seebohm Report, paras. 302-4.
7   John Rex & Robert Moore, Race, community and conflict: a study of Sparkbrook (London, 1967).
8   Cullingworth, 'The measurement of housing need'.
9   Ibid.
10 Shelter is a voluntary organisation designed primarily to raise money for use in dealing with housing problems. In addition, it has taken on a major role as a ginger group seeking to influence government action in this field.
11 Maud Report, vol. 3, chaps. 1-2.
12 Layton, Building by local authorities, pp. 37-8.
13 Royal Commission on Local Government, p. 42.
14 See for example various comments on the Park Hill development in Sheffield, and the Ronan Point reactions.
15 For example the protracted withholding of rent increases by Greater London Council tenants.

Chapter 7   PERSONAL SOCIAL SERVICES, pp. 71-86

1   Ministry of Health, National Health Service, The Administrative Structure of the Medical and Related Services in England and Wales (London, 1968).
2   Seebohm Report, para. 3.
3   Ibid. Appendix H.
4   Ibid. para. 182.
5   Ibid. para. 127.
6   Palumbro & Williams, 'Predictors of public policy', pp. 80-1
7   Seebohm Report, chap. XIV.
8   Parker, Local health and welfare services.
9   Robert R. Alford & Harry Scoble, Bureaucracy and participation (Chicago, 1969).
10 Seebohm Report, Appendix H.
11 Ibid. paras. 126-9.
12 See Davies, Social needs and resources.
13 Ibid.
14 Ibid.
15 Wildavsky, Politics of the budgetary process.
16 Seebohm Report, Appendix H.
17 See Royal Commission on Local Government in England and Wales, Research Studies.

Chapter 8   POLICE AND FIRE, pp. 87-97

1   For an example of the possibilities of such work see James Q. Wilson, Varieties of police behaviour (London, 1969).
2   See for example Home Office, Working Parties on Equipment and on Operational Efficiency and Management (London, 1966).
3   See Fire Protection Directory (London, 1969).

4   Ben Whittaker, **The Police** (Harmondsworth, 1966).
5   See for example Brian Jackson, **Working class community** (London,
    1968).
6   Bollens, **Exploring the metropolitan community,** pp. 339-40.
7   Factories, office blocks, hospitals and the like.
8   Whittaker, **The Police.**
9   Ibid.

Chapter 9   LIBRARIES, pp. 98-103

1   Ministry of Education, **The Structure of the Public Library Service in
    England and Wales,** Cmnd. 660 (London, 1959).

Chapter 10   LOCAL RATES, pp. 104-9

1   The current system provides an element of subsidy to alleviate the
    impact of rate increases on domestic rate-payers. For a brief account
    of the system, see M. Stonefrost in the **Municipal Year Book, 1968.**
2   See Bealey & Bartholomew, 'The local elections in Newcastle-under-
    Lyme, May 1958'.

Chapter 11   CONCLUSIONS, pp. 110-22

1   Griffith, **Central departments and local authorities.**
2   Sharpe, **Voting in cities,** chap. 1.
3   Birkenhead has been controlled by the Labour Party since 1949 and still
    is in 1969, due to almost total control by Labour of Aldermanic places.
    It displays all the hallmarks of tight party control and these are overtly
    acknowledged in council. At the same time, it levies a low rate by com-
    parison with similar County Boroughs and service expenditure is equally
    low.
4   The regularity of both turn-out and party variation across county
    boroughs is very well established. See Sharpe, **Voting in cities,** chap. 13.
5   Gregory, 'Local elections and the "role of anticipated reactions"'.
6   See Boyle, **Equalisation and the future of local government finance.**
7   See, for instance, Moser & Scott, **British towns** and Charles R. Adrian &
    Oliver P. Williams, **Four cities** (Philadelphia, 1963)

Select Bibliography

BOOKS

Adrian, Charles R. (ed.), Social science and community action. East Lansing, Institute for Community Development and Services, 1960.
  & Oliver P. Williams, Four cities. Philadelphia, University of Pennsylvania Press, 1965.

Agger, Robert E., Daniel Goldrich & Bert E. Swanson, The rulers and the ruled. New York, Wiley, 1964.

Alford, Robert R. & Harry Scoble, Bureaucracy and participation. Chicago, Rand Mcnally, 1969.

Almond, Gabriel A. & Sidney Verba, The civic culture. Princeton, Princeton University Press, 1963.

Banfield, Edward C. & James Q. Wilson, City politics. Cambridge, Mass., Harvard University Press, 1963.

Bealey, F., J. Blondel & W. McCann, Constituency politics. London, Faber, 1965.

Birch, A. H., Small town politics. London, Oxford University Press, 1959.

Benham, H., Two cheers for the town hall. London, Hutchinson, 1964

Bloomberg, Warner, Jr & Morris H. Sunshine, Suburban power structures and public education. Syracuse, Syracuse University Press, 1963.

Bollens, John C. (ed.), Exploring the metropolitan community. Berkeley, University of California Press, 1961.

Boyle, Lawrence, Equalisation and the future of local government finance. London, Oliver & Boyd, 1966.

Brazer, Harvey E., City expenditures in the United States. Washington, National Bureau of Economic Research, 1959.

Brennan, T., E. W. Cooney & H. Pollins, Social change in South West Wales. London, Watts, 1954.

Buehrig, Edward H. (ed.), Essays in political science. Bloomington, Indiana University Press, 1966.

Bulpitt, J. G., Party politics in English local government. London, Longmans, 1967.

Chester, D. N., Central and local government. London, Macmillan, 1951.

Cullingworth, J. B., Housing and local government. London, Allen & Unwin, 1966.

Dahl, Robert A., Who governs? New Haven, Yale University Press, 1961.

Davies, B. P., Social needs and resources in local services. London, Michael Joseph, 1968.

Drummond, J. M., The finance of local government. London, Allen & Unwin, 1962.

Dye Thomas R., Politics, economics and the public: policy outcomes in the American States. Chicago, Rand McNally, 1967.

Green, L. P., Provincial metropolis. London, Allen & Unwin, 1959.

Griffith, J. A. G., Central departments and local authorities. London, Allen & Unwin, 1966.

Hadden, Jeffrey K. & Edgar F. Borgatta, American cities: their social characteristics. Chicago, Rand McNally, 1965.

Hart, W. O., Introduction to the law of local government and administration (8th edn.). London, Butterworths, 1969.

Headrick, T. E., The town clerk in English local government. London, Allen & Unwin, 1962.

Hicks, J. R. & U. K., Standards of local expenditure. London, Cambridge University Press, 1943.

The incidence of local rates in Great Britain. London, Cambridge University Press, 1943.

Hunter, Floyd, Community power structure. Chapel Hill, N.C., University of North Carolina Press, 1953.

Institute of Municipal Treasurers and Accountants, Local expenditure and exchequer grants. London, 1956.

Jackson, R. M., The machinery of local government. London, Macmillan, 1965.

Layton, Elizabeth, Building by local authorities. London, Allen & Unwin, 1961.

Lee, J. M., Social leaders and public persons. London, Oxford University Press, 1963.

Mackenzie, W. J. M., Theories of local government. London, London School of Economics, 1961.

Marshall, A. H., Financial administration in local government. London, Allen & Unwin, 1960.

Moser, C. A. & Wolf Scott, British towns. London, Oliver & Boyd, 1961.

Parker, Julia, Local health and welfare services. London, Allen & Unwin, 1965.

Parkinson, M. H., The Labour Party and the organisation of secondary education, 1918-65. London, Routledge & Kegan Paul, 1970.

Polsby, Nelson W., Community power and political theory. New Haven, Yale University Press, 1970.

Rees, A. M. & T. A. Smith, Town councillors. London, Acton Society Trust, 1964.

Rex, John & Robert Moore, Race, community and conflict: a study of Sparkbrook. London, Oxford University Press, 1967.

Rhodes, Gerald, Town government in South East England. London, London School of Economics, 1967.

Robson, William A., Local government in crisis. London, Allen & Unwin, 1966.

Royal Institute of Public Administration, New sources of local revenue. London, Allen & Unwin, 1956.

Schnore, Leo F. & Henry Fagin, Urban research and policy planning. Beverley Hills, Calif., Sage Publications, 1967.

Sharpe, L. J., Why local democracy? London, Fabian Tract 361, 1965.

A metropolis votes. London, London School of Economics, 1962.

(ed.), Voting in cities. London, Macmillan, 1967.

145

Stacey, M., **Tradition and change.** London, Oxford University Press, 1960.
Stanyer, Jeffrey, **County government in England and Wales.** London, Routledge & Kegan Paul, 1967.
Whittaker, Ben, **The Police.** Harmondsworth, Penguin, 1966.
Wildavsky, Aaron, **Politics of the budgetary process.** Boston, Little Brown, 1964.
Williams, Oliver P., Harold Herman, Charles S. Liebman & Thomas R. Dye, **Surburban differences and metropolitan policies: a Philadelphia story.** Philadelphia, University of Pennsylvania Press, 1965.
Wilson, James Q., **Varieties of police behaviour.** London, Oxford University Press, 1969.
(ed.), **City politics and public policy.** New York, Wiley, 1968.
Wood, Robert C., **1400 governments.** New York, Doubleday, 1964.

ARTICLES

Bachrach, Peter & Morton S. Baratz, 'Decisions and non-decisions: an analytical framework', **American Political Science Review,** vol. 57 (1963).
'Two faces of power', **American Political Science Review,** vol. 56 (1962).
Bealey, F. & D. J. Bartholomew, 'The local elections in Newcastle-under-Lyme, May 1958', **British Journal of Sociology,** XIII, 3 & 4 (1962).
Boaden, Noel T. & Robert R. Alford, 'Sources of diversity in English local government decisions', **Public Administration** (Summer 1969).
Cullingworth, J. B., 'The measurement of housing need', **British Journal of Sociology,** IX, 4 (Dec. 1958).
Davies, Bleddyn & V. Williamson, 'School meals - short fall and poverty'. **Social and Economic Administration,** II, 1 (1968).
Davis, Otto, M. A. H. Dempster & A. Wildavsky, 'A theory of the budgetary process', **American Political Science Review,** vol. LX (Sept. 1966).
Dawson, Richard E. & James A. Robinson, 'Inter-party competition, economic variables and welfare policies in the American States', **The Journal of Politics,** vol. 25 (1963).
Froman, Lewis Jr, 'An analysis of public policies in cities', **The Journal of Politics,** vol. 29 (1967).
Gregory, R. G., 'Local elections and the "role of anticipated reaction" ', **Political Studies,** XVIII, 1 (March 1969).
Hofferbert, Richard, I., 'The relations between public policy and some structural and environmental variables in the American States', **American Political Science Review,** vol. 60 (March 1966).
Kaufman, Herbert, 'The next step in case studies', **Public Administration Review,** vol. 18 (1958).
Mack, Raymond W. & Denis C. McEllarth, 'Urban social differentiation and the allocation of resources', **Annals of the American Academy of Political Science** (1964).
Miller, Delbert C., 'Decision making cliques in community power structures', **American Journal of Sociology** (1957).

Oliver, F. R., 'The regressiveness of local rates as a form of taxation', Social and Economic Administration, I, 2(1967).
Ollerenshaw, Kathleen, 'Sharing responsibility', Public Administration (1962).
Ostrom, Vincent, Charles M. Tiebout & Robert Warren, 'The organisation of government in metropolitan areas: a theoretical inquiry', American Political Science Review, LV, 4 (Dec. 1961).
Palumbro, Dennis J. & Oliver P. Williams, 'Predictors of public policy: The case of local public health', Urban Affairs Quarterly, II, 4 (June 1967).
Polsby, Nelson W., 'Three problems in the analysis of community power', American Sociological Review, vol. 24 (1959).
Sady, E. J., 'The need for comparative studies on practical problems of urban administration', Comparative administrative Group Conference (April 1966).
Sharkansky, Ira, 'Government expenditures and public services in the American States', American Political Science Review, LXI, 4 (Dec. 1967).
Sleeman J., 'Variation of educational costs in Scotland', Scottish Educational Journal, 21 June 1963.
'Education costs and local government structure in Scotland', Scottish Journal of Political Economy, vol. 12 (1965).
Thornhill, W., 'Agreements between political parties in local government matters', Political Studies, V, 1(1957).
Tiebout, Charles, M., 'A pure theory of local expenditures', Journal of Political Economy, vol. 64 (1956).
Wiseman, H. V., 'Local government in Leeds', Public Administration, 41, 1 & 2 (1963).
Wolfinger, Raymond, 'A plea for a decent burial', American Sociological Review, vol. 27 (1962).

GOVERNMENT PUBLICATIONS

Allen, R. G. D., Report of the Allen Committee of Inquiry into the Impact of Rates on Households. Cmnd. 2582, H.M.S.O., London, 1965.
Department of Education and Science, Standards of Public Library Service in England and Wales. H.M.S.O., London, 1961.
Home Office, Working Party on Operational Efficiency and Management. H.M.S.O., London, 1966.
Working Party on Equipment. H.M.S.O., London, 1966.
Ministry of Education, The Structure of the Public Library Service in England and Wales. Cmnd. 660, H.M.S.O., London, 1959.
Ministry of Health, National Health Service, The Administrative Structure of the Medical and Related Services in England and Wales. H.M.S.O., London, 1968.
Ministry of Housing and Local Government, Management of Local Government, vols. 1-5. H.M.S.O., London, 1967.
Staffing of Local Government. H.M.S.O., London, 1967.
National Board for Prices and Incomes, Report no. 62: Increases in Rents of Local Authority Housing. H.M.S.O., London, 1968.

Report of the Local Government Boundary Commission. H.M.S.O., London, 1948.

Report of the Working Party on Social Workers in the Local Authority Health and Welfare Services. H.M.S.O., London, 1959.

Royal Commission on Local Government in England and Wales, 1966, Report, vol. 1, 1969.

Research Study no. 3: Institute of Social and Economic Research, University of York, **Economies of Scale in Local Government Services.** H.M.S.O., London, 1968.

Research Study no. 4: Local Government Operational Research Unit, **Performance and Size of Local Educational Authorities.** H.M.S.O., London, 1968.

Research Study no. 5: Government Social Survey, **Local Authority Services and the Characteristics of Administrative Areas.** H.M.S.O., London, 1968.

Research Study no. 7: Institute of Local Government Studies, University of Birmingham, **Aspects of Administration in a Large Local Authority.** H.M.S.O., London, 1968.

Research Study no. 9: Research Services Ltd, **Community Attitudes Survey.** H.M.S.O., London, 1969.

Research Study no. 10: The Institute of Local Government Studies, University of Birmingham, **Administration in a Large Local Authority, a Comparison with other County Boroughs.** H.M.S.O., London, 1969.

Seebohm, F., **Report of the Committee on Local Authority and Allied Personal Social Services.** H.M.S.O., London, 1968.

Skeffington, A., **People and planning.** H.M.S.O., London, 1969.

Index

Mackenzie, W. J. M., 6
Maud Committee, 44, 73
Merthyr Tydfil County Borough,
  16, 18
Moser, C. A., 8
museums, 39

needs, xiii, 21-3, 28-30, 46-7, 60-1,
  67, 72, 88-9, 98-100, 104, 110-12

officials, 25, 32, 44, 74, 78, 85, 86,
  89, 90, 100-1, 105, 112, 121
Oldham County Borough, 18

packageability of services, 39
Parker, Julia, 14
parks, 40, 41
Planning Department, 36
police service, 37-8, 40, 41, 42,
  chap. 8 passim, 117-19
Prices and Incomes Board, 59-60, 67
public attitudes, 26, 33-4, 44, 86, 105,
  112;
  involvement, xiv, 5, 7, 80, 115

rate, general, 3, 4, 29, 34, chap. 10;
  subsidy, 67-70
regional variations in services,
  117, 119
resources, xiii, 21, 26-7, 34, 41, 54,
  62-3, 67, 74-5, 90, 101, 105, 115-
  16

Robson, W. A., 2, 3, 11, 12
Rochdale County Borough, 18

Rossi, P., 9, 11
Royal Commission on Local
  Government, xiii, 11, 12, 63, 115
Royal Institute of Public Administra-
  tion, 12
Rutland County Council, 5, 6

Scott, W., 8
Seebohm Report, 23, 71-4, 78. 83
Shelter, 62
social services, chap. 7, 119-20
Solihull County Borough, 45-6
South Shields County Borough, 18

Town Clerk's Department, 36
transport, public, 39
Treasurer's Department, 36, 62, 67
Tynemouth County Borough, 16

variables, see under dispositions,
  needs, resources of need, 111
voluntary organisations, 73-4, 121

Wakefield County Borough, 16
Warrington County Borough, 16
welfare service, 14, 16, 18, 33, 37,
  39, 40, 41, 42, chap. 7 passim,
  117-19
West Hartlepool County Borough,
  16, 18
Whittaker, B., 88, 96
Wildavsky, A., 37
Wilson, J. Q., 8, 9, 11
Wood, R. C., 37
Worcester County Borough, 16

KING ALFRED'S COLLEGE
LIBRARY